GERMAN PARATROOPS

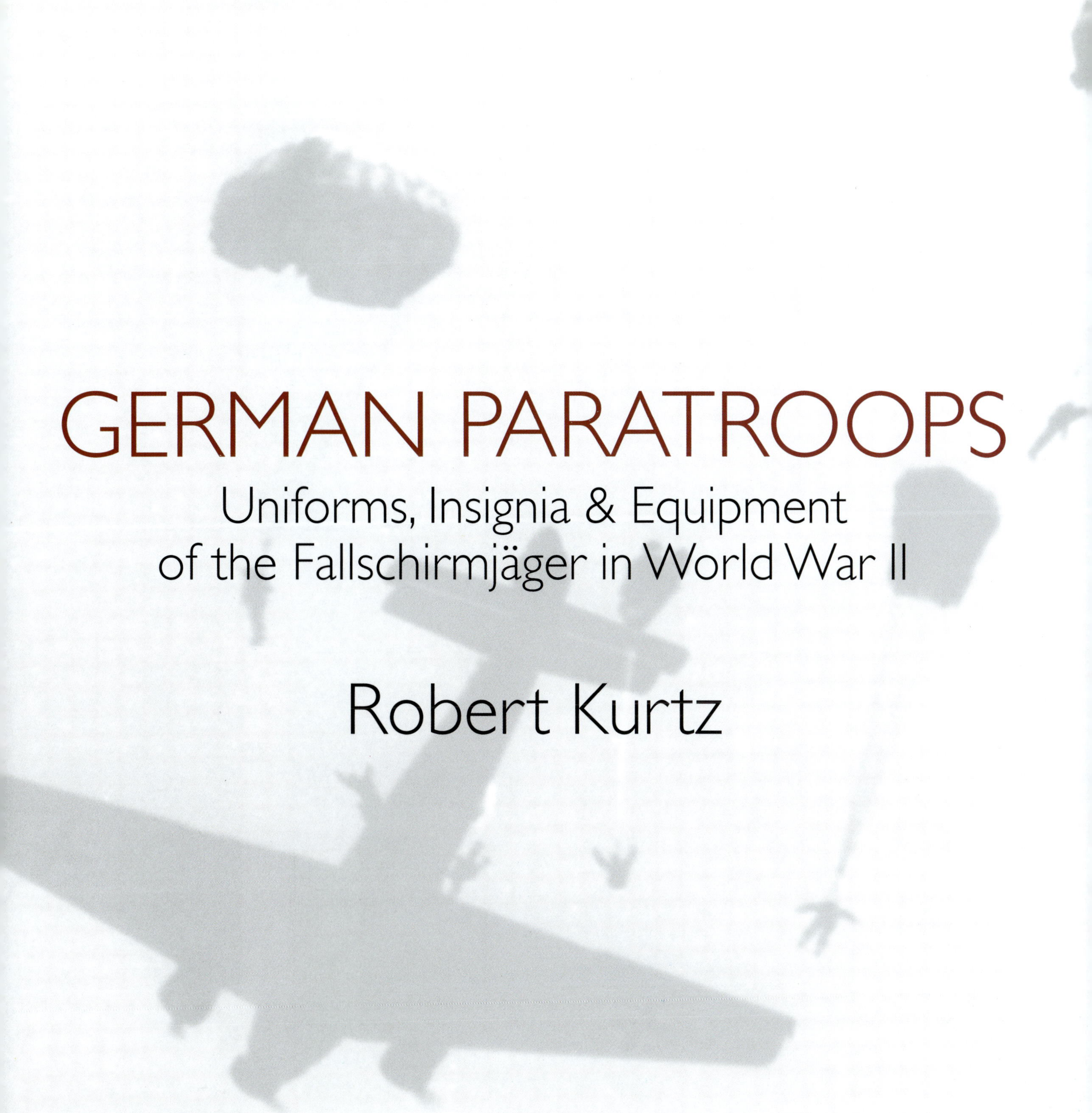

GERMAN PARATROOPS

Uniforms, Insignia & Equipment of the Fallschirmjäger in World War II

Robert Kurtz

Schiffer Military History
Atglen, PA

ACKNOWLEDGMENTS

The publisher wishes to thank Chris Mason, Bill Shea and Willi Zahn who generously opened their collections for this book, and who graciously gave of their time, expertise and hospitality. Their participation and enthusiasm made this book possible.

Also, thanks to Beth C. Beck, Ken Ettin, Jack Hatter, Raoul Ingröch, Mick Linz, Jon Maguire, Chris Mybro, Brana Radovic, Matthew Reinert, Guy Richardson, Roger Sodanowicz, Charles Woolley, and Mark Yerger for their support, and to the staff of the Bundesarchiv/Bildarchiv, Koblenz for their assistance.

Photography and book design by Robert Biondi

Library of Congress Control Number: 99-67578

ISBN: 978-0-7643-1040-9
Printed in China

Schiffer Books are available at special discounts for bulk purchases for sales promotions or premiums. Special editions, including personalized covers, corporate imprints, and excerpts can be created in large quantities for special needs. For more information contact the publisher:

Published by Schiffer Publishing Ltd.
4880 Lower Valley Road
Atglen, PA 19310
Phone: (610) 593-1777; Fax: (610) 593-2002
E-mail: Info@schifferbooks.com
For the largest selection of fine reference books on this and related subjects, please visit our web site at
www.schifferbooks.com

In Europe, Schiffer books are distributed by
Bushwood Books
6 Marksbury Ave.
Kew Gardens
Surrey TW9 4JF England
Phone: 44 (0) 20 8392 8585; Fax: 44 (0) 20 8392 9876
E-mail: info@bushwoodbooks.co.uk
Website: www.bushwoodbooks.co.uk

This book may be purchased from the publisher.
Include $5.00 for shipping. Please try your bookstore first.
You may write for a free catalog.
We are always looking for people to write books on new and related subjects. If you have an idea for a book please contact us at the above address.

Contents

Foreword

World War II was much different from the First World War in many ways. Each time a war between two forces breaks out, new techniques, strategies, innovations and equipment all become by-products of the conflict. The Second World War was certainly no exception to this. Weapons such as airplanes, submarines and tanks, which cut their teeth in the "Great War", developed into strategic weapons in World War II.

However, the concept of soldiers falling from the sky in a planned location was unheard of. The mere thought of "shock troops" assaulting a location behind the enemy's position was pure fantasy. But near the close of the 1930s and with the clouds of war gathering on the horizon, all of the future belligerents began experimenting with this concept. Employing airborne troops effectively became a necessary and vital weapon in their arsenal of warfare.

Many in-depth books have been written on the successes and failures of these mighty warriors and many histories have detailed what great sacrifices these soldiers endured. This book focuses on the variety of clothing and specialized equipment used by the German Fallschirmjäger. Never before used gear, from head to foot, was designed, developed, tested and issued to these soldiers. Even as the war dragged on this new equipment was changed again and again to reflect the differences in seasons, terrain and the enemy.

I have collected military memorabilia for forty years and have been very fortunate over the years to speak with hundreds of United States veterans who served their country during World War II. Many of these veterans returned from the war with "booty", and in many cases these souvenirs came right off the battlefield. Their philosophy of "to the victor goes the spoils" certainly was true of virtually every G.I. who played "capture the flag" as a youngster. They brought home everything that wasn't nailed down and in some cases, even the nails didn't stop them.

My interest in this topic and the story behind it continued to grow throughout the years. The information gathered from American GIs was sketchy and I longed for more details. This is where the written and pictorial word has become so valuable. As stated before, many books have been written on these topics. This book strives to go one step further. Shown here are some of the best possible examples of Fallschirmjäger specialized equipment. These artifacts have been gathered from some of the most advanced collectors of paratrooper gear and are pictured in great detail for viewing and educational purposes. This reference provides the reader with not only visual information but also insightful written details explaining the items. The book is not intended to completely cover every aspect of paratrooper ephemera. It is hoped that it will serve as a conduit to motivate the reader to have a basic understanding of the special place these soldiers held in the big picture we refer to as the Second World War.

Bill Shea
"The Ruptured Duck"
December 1999

Chapter One

Uniforms
Smocks, Tunics, Trousers

Unissued example of a second model Luftwaffe green step-in smock. This particular smock is dated July 1938, was manufactured by the firm of "Schultz" in Berlin, and is sized "IIb", or medium regular. This smock portrays the exact configuration of the smocks worn by many of the Fallschirmtruppen during the Kreta campaign. (Willi Zahn)

This back view shows that the standard second model smocks did not have the entrenching tool retaining loop and the flare pistol holster. Second model step-in smocks which were modified after the Kreta campaign into open front configuration usually had these features added. (Willi Zahn)

Close up of the machine stitched Luftwaffe eagle. Note the chalk lines which were probably drawn by the tailor to line up the eagle before application. The four front pockets were added at a later date – this was a modification done after the campaign in Holland 1940, after it was determined that outside pockets were needed. Smocks made before that date sometimes had the pockets added, whereas smocks made after that time usually had them factory applied as a normal feature. (Willi Zahn)

Right side view showing the side zippers and details of the inner and outer cuff. These side access zippers were standard on second model smocks, and were designed to allow access to the equipment or uniform worn under the smock. The wearing of equipment under the smock was a standard practice during the early years of the Fallschirmtruppen. The wind cuff inside the sleeve is made of cotton and the snaps are marked "PRYM 6". (Willi Zahn)

Training photos of paratrooper in Luftwaffe green step-in smock with RZ1 parachute. Note parachute carrying bags.

A good early portrait of a Fallschirmjäger wearing the so-called "jump school smock," the early olive green version without pockets. He is wearing side lace boots, holds a double decal helmet, and has a dark blue Luftwaffe "combat" belt buckle. (C. Mason)

Detail of the factory-applied breast eagle, embroidered on the early flecked-green material. (C. Mason)

An example of the splinter-pattern camouflage jump smock using the older, flecked green cotton which is overprinted with the camouflage pattern. This comparatively rare variant is often referred to by collectors as the "splinter-on-olive" smock. (C. Mason)

Another example of the splinter-pattern camouflage paratrooper smock, worn over an officer's Fliegerbluse. (C. Mason)

This smock's eagle is also on early flecked-green material. The tight stitching pattern is typical of the time-intensive quality of earlier production smocks. (C. Mason)

An example of the early pattern of the Fliegerbluse made without pockets, this one worn by an Oberstleutnant of the paratroops. (C. Mason)

Right: This detail of the Fliegerbluse shows the early officer's breast eagle and the application of the cloth version of the German Cross in Gold. (C. Mason)

This rear view of the parade harness also shows details of the integral flare gun holster on the right hip. Period photos indicate this design feature was seldom, if ever, used for the intended purpose. (C. Mason)

For ceremonies and parades, Fallschirmjäger often wore the jump smock with Fliegerbluse, shirt and tie, and a parachute harness with the parachute containment bag removed. (C. Mason)

A portrait photograph of an unknown Fallschirmjäger. He is wearing the splinter pattern smock and helmet cover with hooks, Fallschirmjäger trousers, the RZ1 ceremonial harness, front lace boots, paratrooper gloves and his Fallschirmschützenabzeichen. Note the blue polka dot scarf favored by Fallschirmjäger Regiment 1. (C. Mason)

Rear view showing holster set up and use of the flare pistol.

Close up showing the stainless steel zipper for the insert pocket. Note the detail of the camouflage pattern and the distinctive camouflage backed, machine embroidered Luftwaffe eagle which has been zig-zag applied to the smock. Also shown is a stainless steel zipper with brown leather pull.

Third Model Luftwaffe "Splinter" Pattern Camouflage Paratrooper Smock. This has been "late wartime" converted to a field division smock by trimming approximately 12" off the bottom. Such modifications were occasionally made in the field to salvage a damaged garment or to suit individual preference. (Collection of Captain Stuart Lockhart, USMC)

Interior lining and markings. The white linen liner has the RBnr contract issue number and size markings (IIb).

Late-war third model smock in the Luftwaffe "splinter" pattern. By now the four front pockets were a standard feature, as was the five button open front construction. Lessons learned during the Kreta campaign called for the step-in model to be replaced by this model which could be more easily removed. (Willi Zahn)

This view shows the addition of the entrenching tool retaining loop on the lower left, and the flare pistol holster on the lower right. Both of these features were standard on most third model smocks. (Willi Zahn)

The machine stitched cotton backed eagle encountered on many splinter smocks is shown here. These eagles were sewn on at the factory before the pockets were attached to the smock. (Willi Zahn)

This photograph of a Fallschirmjäger victory parade in Goslar after their return from Crete in 1941 shows the Oberleutnant and Oberfeldwebel on the left were issued the new splinter pattern camouflage jump smocks for the operation, while the troops continue to wear the plain olive-green smock. The Oberfeldwebel has camouflaged his helmet. The man third from right still has the national colors shield on his helmet. His size 71 helmet shell, the largest size shell which was produced, stands out in a crowd. (C. Mason)

Inside view showing the construction of the pocket linings, flare holster lining, waist adjustment tape and the armpit. (Willi Zahn)

Close up of flare pistol holster. This view also shows the right side adjustment tab with snap used to narrow the waist, a feature standard on third model smocks. (Willi Zahn)

This third model splinter smock was produced in January of 1944 and represents the standard type of smock worn by the Fallschirmtruppen during 1944. (Willi Zahn)

The standard features of the third model smock are again evident in this photo. (Willi Zahn)

Note that the side waist adjustment tabs are made out of water pattern material, an interesting feature of this smock. On many smocks, especially late-war production, the use of fabric in a different camouflage pattern, or just a variation of the same pattern, is sometimes encountered. (Willi Zahn)

Another type of cotton backed breast eagle encountered on smocks. As was common practice for Luftwaffe clothing that had zippers, a leather tab was sewn to the zipper pull. (Willi Zahn)

This view shows the construction of the hidden button hole found on third model smocks. This feature is extremely well-made as evidenced by the reinforcement stitches and the lining. Also present in this photo are two of the five glass buttons used to button the smock. (Willi Zahn)

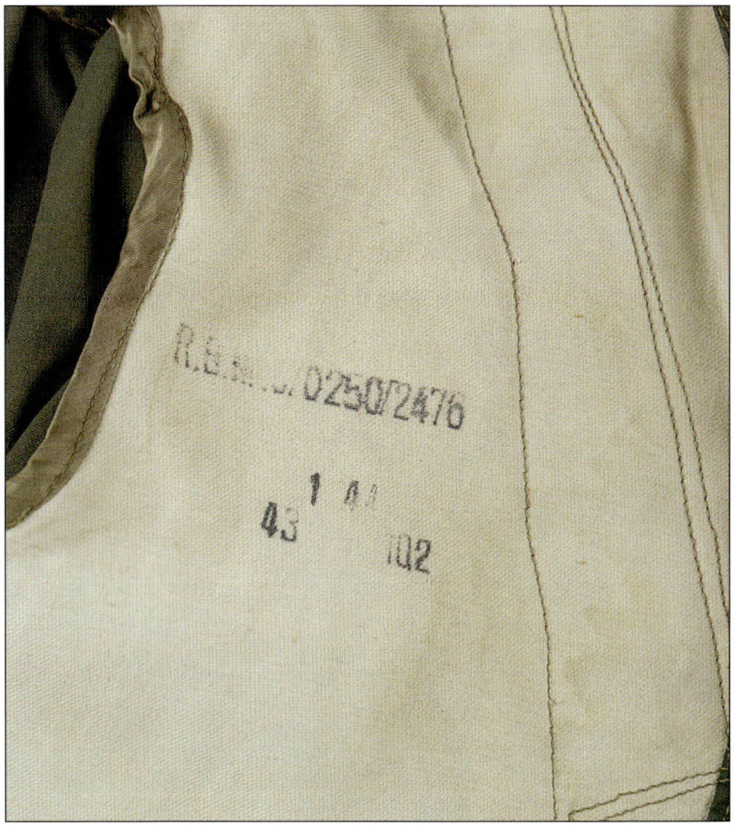

The markings on the back of the left upper pocket lining. The R.B.Nr indicates the manufacturer of the smock, and the other numbers indicate the date of manufacture (1 44) and the size markings. (Willi Zahn)

Paratroops wearing second model splinter step-in smocks. Note mix of Army and Luftwaffe breast eagles, and Army belt buckles.

A squad of Fallschirmjäger taking a break during a late winter exercise in northern Germany sometime after Crete. They are all wearing splinter pattern camouflage smocks. The man in the foreground still has a national colors shield on his helmet. Double decal helmets are spotted from time to time in period photographs taken as late as 1944. (C. Mason)

Rear view of this unusual variation. Note that the fabric used for both the flare pistol holster and the entrenching tool is slightly different in color and fabric than the rest of the smock. This may indicate that those features were added at a later date, or they used the fabric which later replaced the splinter printed over the early green fabric. (Willi Zahn)

This early example of a third model splinter smock is dated 1942. What makes this particular pattern unusual is that the splinter pattern is printed on the green fabric used for the construction of earlier green second model step-in smocks. (Willi Zahn)

This smock features an eagle with the standard Luftwaffe blue/gray wool backing. Wool backed eagles are sometimes encountered on both 1942 and 1943 dated splinter pattern smocks. (Willi Zahn)

The stamping indicates that this smock was made in September of 1942 and is sized 1 B, or small regular. Early smocks had the manufacturer's name present before the introduction of the RB Nr codes. (Willi Zahn)

Close up view of the inside of the 1942 dated smock showing construction of the button holes. Note the different colors of thread used in the construction of the early green fabric which was used in the manufacture of most second model green step-in smocks, some second model splinter step-in smocks and some early third model splinter smocks. (Willi Zahn)

Tropical scene showing a mix of Luftwaffe green and splinter smocks. Officer at right wears a Meyer cap.

Photos taken of Fallschirmjäger during early 1945 show that some troopers were issued these ground division smocks, which were much shorter than normal jump smocks. (Willi Zahn)

Luftwaffe ground division smock in the Luftwaffe splinter pattern, which like that of the FJ smocks, is slightly different than the splinter pattern used in Heer (Army) clothing items. This smock is constructed in an "HBT" (hearing bone twill) fabric. (Willi Zahn)

This eagle is on a blue-gray wool material, the type normally encountered on Luftwaffe wool uniforms. As was common practice with most Luftwaffe breast eagles, it is machine zig-zag stitched. (Willi Zahn)

The markings of this example are stamped on the lining of the inside pocket, found on the upper left side of the smock. (Willi Zahn)

Typical water-pattern camouflage jump smock circa 1944. (C. Mason)

This photograph of Gefreiter Otto Asböck illustrates the extent to which uniform regulations were often ignored. He has added dark-piped shoulderboards to his camouflage jump smock. In addition, he has affixed rank gulls to his collar and sewn on both a cloth version of the paratrooper badge (with an unusually dark eagle) and an iron cross ribbon, all unorthodox practices. In addition, instead of wearing either the Infantry Assault Badge or the Luftwaffe Ground Combat Badge (Erdkampfabzeichen) which superceded it, he is wearing both at the same time. To top it off he's wearing an athletic jacket instead of a tunic or shirt visible underneath his smock. Asböck was killed in action in Holland during Operation Market Garden on November 14, 1944. (C. Mason)

Detail of the factory-applied breast eagle. This one is on a thin rayon base material in an olive-green color. (C. Mason)

Rear view. Notice the holster set up for the flare pistol and the fabric loop (on left side) for attaching equipment.

Third Model Luftwaffe "Tan and Water" Pattern Camouflage Paratrooper Jump Smock. Notice the soft dissolving various color transitions from one area to another. The emphasis here was on the color brown. (Collection of Bill Shea, "The Ruptured Duck")

The machine embroidered Luftwaffe eagle is zig-zag machine applied. This example has the white plastic zippers. Stainless steel and zinc zippers were also used.

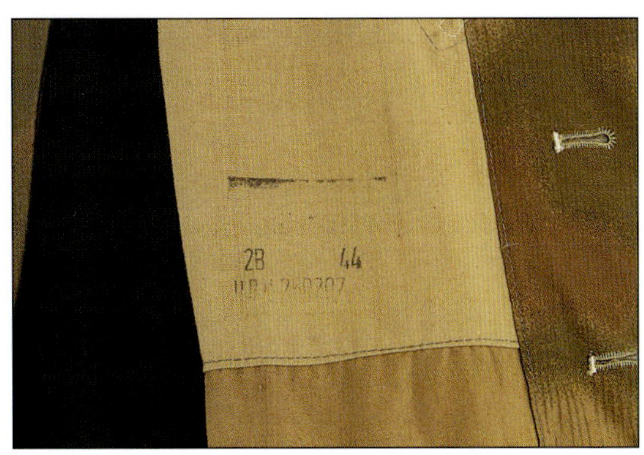

Interior view showing the different interior liner panels and also the ink size stamps and contract number (RB Nr).

This smock was manufactured in November of 1944 and is a third model in water pattern camouflage. The Wehrmacht introduced the water pattern camouflage variation in 1943 as a replacement for the splinter pattern. The splinter pattern smock, however, continued to be the preferred camouflage pattern for veteran Fallschirmtruppen. (Willi Zahn)

The water pattern smock still maintained all the features of the third model smock. This particular example still has the paper manufacturer's tag sewn to the back. (Willi Zahn)

The construction of the flare pistol holster is again visible here. Note the stitch lines of the holster lining which is attached to the inside of the smock. (Willi Zahn)

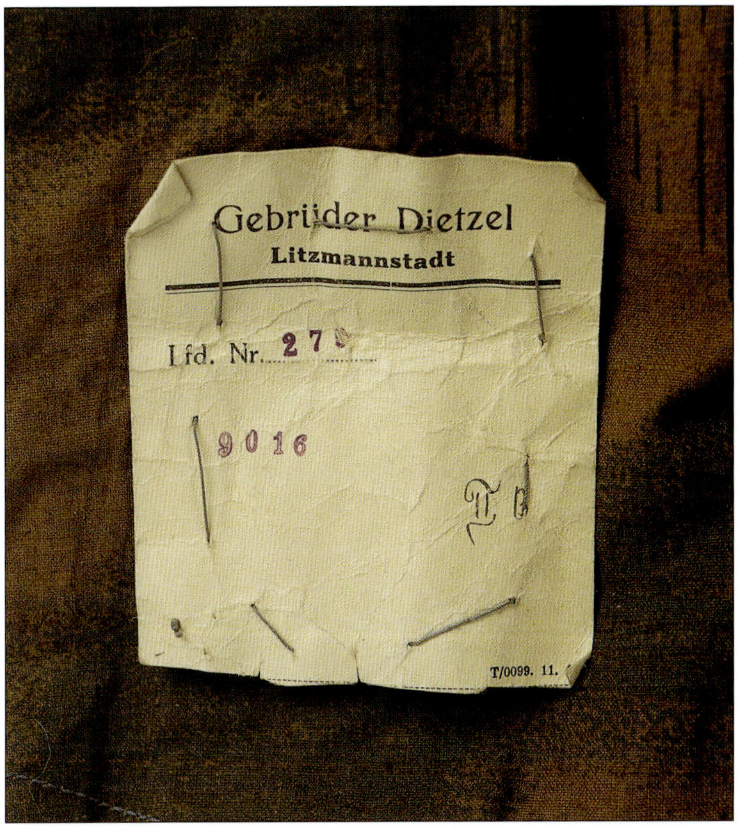

The paper tag which indicates this smock was made by the "Gebrüder Dietzel" company in Litzmannstadt in occupied Poland. The size marking indicates "2b", or medium regular. (Willi Zahn)

The zippers of this particular smock are made of plastic, another common feature of some Luftwaffe clothing. These plastic zippers, made by the firm of "RiRi", are encountered on smocks made in both splinter and water patterns. Note the zipper pull tab made from natural colored leather. (Willi Zahn)

The markings present on the left side pocket lining. Once again the RBNr indicates both the manufacturer and that the smock was made in November of 1944. The size marking of "IIb" is again present. (Willi Zahn)

Third model smocks in the tan and water camouflage pattern were made in numerous color variations. This unusual variation is dated 1944 and was brought home by a veteran of the U.S. 10th Mountain Division, who found it in a Luftwaffe supply depot north of the Po River in 1945. (Willi Zahn)

This smock is manufactured on a very heavy "duck type" cotton. Smocks were made out of numerous weights of cotton fabric. (Willi Zahn)

This machine zig-zag stitched eagle is on a thin blue-gray cotton backing. (Willi Zahn)

Once again the markings indicate the manufacturer in the form of the RB Nr code, the size of "IIb", indicating medium regular, and the year of manufacture, 1944. The off-white fabric is the pocket lining, present on all four pockets. (Willi Zahn)

This smock is constructed of a very thin cotton material and retains all the normal features of a third model smock, despite its very late manufacture.

Another variation to the tan and water pattern dated December 1944. This color combination is more subdued and found on the last issue of third model smocks. (Willi Zahn)

This subdued late-war eagle is on a thin green cotton backing, a common feature of the late-issue smocks. (Willi Zahn)

The five metal dish buttons are another feature of the late-war water pattern smocks. Metal dish buttons are also found on some splinter pattern smocks. (Willi Zahn)

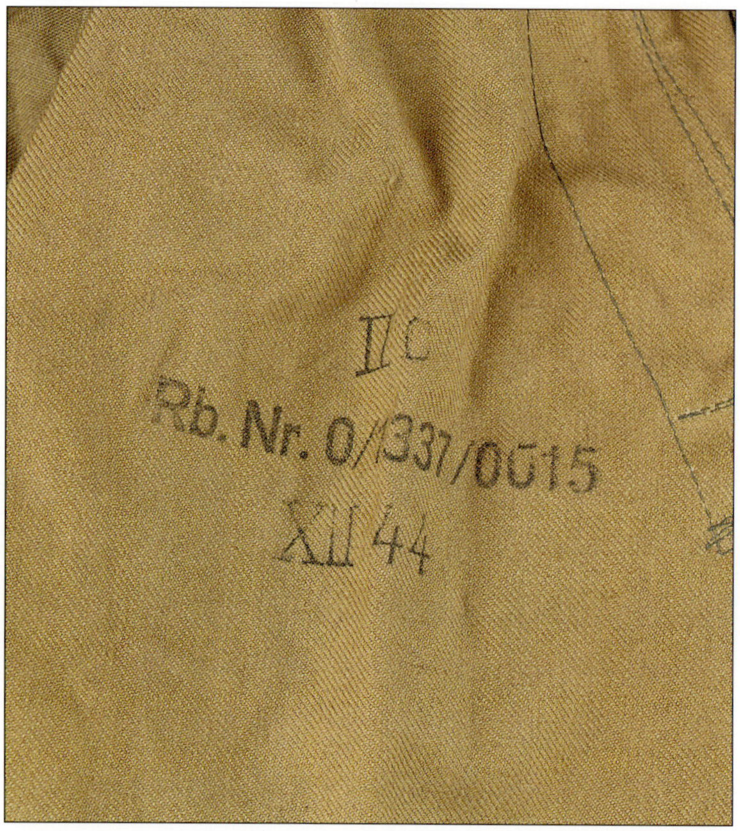

This smock is sized "IIc" or medium long. The "XII" indicates that the smock was manufactured in December of 1944. The markings of "I", "II" or "III" on fallschirmjäger smocks indicate small, medium or large, and the letter "a", "b" or "c" indicates short, regular or long. (Willi Zahn)

Ground division smocks have very little in common with Fallschirmjäger smocks in regards to features, and were not designed for parachute jumping. (Willi Zahn)

This eagle is on a thin green cotton backing, the style commonly found on jump smocks. (Willi Zahn)

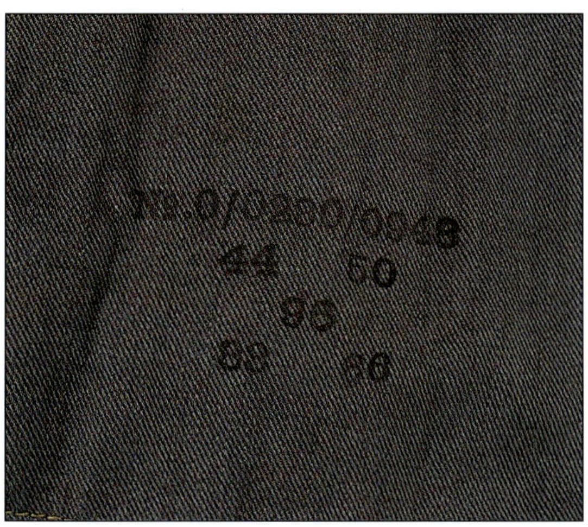

These size markings were very similar to the style encountered in most Wehrmacht tunics. The markings are present on the inside pocket which is found on the upper left side. (Willi Zahn)

Luftwaffe ground division smock in water pattern. Though normally issued to Luftwaffe Field Divisions, these smocks can be seen worn by late-war paratroopers. These smocks do not have hidden buttons, have only two outside pockets, and are set up to take shoulder boards. (Willi Zahn)

German Paratrooper Rig. This rig is distinctively paratrooper from head to toe with its specialized equipment such as camouflage steel helmet, paratrooper smock and ammunition bandoleer. This set up also includes lightweight tropical style trousers with large cargo pocket on the left knee and even the earlier side-lace paratrooper boots. Additionally, standard equipment includes the fighting knife and a pair of Model 1924 stick grenades ("potato mashers"). (Collection of Bill Shea, "The Ruptured Duck")

Rear view. Clearly visible are the camouflage chicken wire helmet and specialized harness, and the tan and water camouflage pattern smock.

Four views representing the general appearance of a member of the 7th Flieger Division during the Crete invasion on May 20, 1941. The smock worn during that campaign was either a green or splinter second model step-in smock. This helmet is an early spanner bolt M38 jump helmet in a smooth dark green-gray finish. Also shown are a pair of Luftwaffe issue MP38/40 magazine pouches which hold six 32-round magazines, an aluminum Luftwaffe buckle, a pair of pre-war lightweight brown leather Luftwaffe y-straps, brown leather belt, a P08 (Luger) holster, a M24 stick grenade, a Luftwaffe issue bread bag and an early issue canteen with black painted cup. (Willi Zahn)

Four views representing the general appearance of a member of either the 2nd, 3rd or 5th Fallschirmjäger Division in the summer of 1944 during the Normandy campaign. This third model smock is in the splinter pattern, which was the standard for the Normandy campaign, though others where also worn. This helmet is the standard mid-war spanner bolt helmet in a rough dark green-gray paint, which has had several pieces of heavy wire attached to hold camouflage. Also shown is a late-war issue FJ gas mask bag, MP38/40 magazine pouches, M24 stick grenade, P08 holster, lightweight y-straps, late-war canteen and cup, Luftwaffe issue bread bag and Luftwaffe steel buckle in blue-gray. (Willi Zahn)

Four views representing the general appearance of a member of either the 1st or 4th Fallschirmjäger Division in the summer of 1944 during the Italian campaign. This third model smock is in water pattern, though the Fallschirmtruppen also wore the green and splinter pattern smocks in this theater as well, in both the second or third model. This helmet is a standard spanner bolt model which has had a heavy coat of tan paint sprayed on. Also shown are a pair of late-war binoculars in ordnance tan, a set of late-war bandoleers in olive-tan, a Luftwaffe tropical belt and buckle, a tropical bread bag with web fittings, a tropical canteen with olive-tan painted canteen cup, a P08 holster and a M24 stick grenade. (Willi Zahn)

Paratroops in winter dress. Note camouflage helmets.

F.A. Freiherr von der Heydte, shown here in the rank of Major, wearing four pocket tunic. Note both the Afrika and Kreta cuff titles on left sleeve. (Von der Heydte)

Oberleutnant Albert Meyer, killed in action in North Africa in 1943. He is wearing the adjutant's aiguillette in addition to his combat awards. (C. Mason)

Tailor made uniform tunic (Waffenrock) in the rank of Oberleutnant. (Willi Zahn)

Luftwaffe Four Pocket Service Tunic for a paratrooper Obergefreiter (Senior Corporal) as designated by the three metal gulls on the collar tabs and double chevron on the left sleeve. The yellow piping around the collar and shoulder boards plus the color of the collar tabs identify this soldier as being from either a Flight or Paratrooper unit. The Paratrooper badge on the left breast area clearly identifies this blouse as belonging to a Fallschirmjäger. (Collection of Bill Shea, "The Ruptured Duck")

Flyer's blouse (Fliegerbluse) in the rank of Feldwebel. This particular example is dated 1943. The collar tabs, breast eagle and NCO collar tress are all machine sewn on the tunic. (Willi Zahn)

1940 dated flying blouse (Fliegerbluse) in the rank of Obergefreiter. The rank chevrons are on the middle of the left sleeve, but can not be seen in this photo. The fliegerbluse was the standard tunic worn by Fallschirmjäger under their jump smock. (Willi Zahn)

Close-up view of Gefreiter Lippmann's tunic shows the enlisted Fallschirmjäger Regiment 1 cufftitle, the parade belt and the Luftwaffe yellow triangular cufflink in his dress shirt. (C. Mason)

This interior view of the Lippmann tunic shows his laundry label (written in ink on the reverse side of a Fallschirm-Infanterie-Bataillon label, readable using a mirror) and the correct unit markings along the lapel for a Fallschirmjäger-issued garment, in this case, 6. Kompanie, Fallschirmjäger Regiment 1. (C. Mason)

The dress Tuchrock of Gefreiter (later Hauptfeldwebel) Erwin Lippmann. Originally an army paratrooper, Lippmann won the German Cross in Gold in 1944 for gallantry at Monte Cassino. (C. Mason)

Page 46: Side view of Gefreiter Lippmann's tunic showing his badges, awards and tunic details. (C. Mason)

-Jäger Rgt.

1941 dated Luftwaffe tropical tunic in blue-gray cotton. As most tropical clothing is in tan, these tunics where not widely issued. The web belt is also blue-gray, and was picked up by an Australian veteran in North Africa. The buckle also has a blue-gray web tab and is dated 1941. (Willi Zahn)

The assault gun tunic of Sanitäts-Unteroffizier Gerhard Volkmann, who was assigned to Fallschirm-Sturmgeschütz-Brigade 12. (C. Mason)

Right: Side view of Unteroffizier Volkmann's tunic. The use of a metal shoulderboard device as a substitute for the cloth sleeve specialty insignia and the unusual position of his awards on the tunic are both visible in the period photograph of Volkmann wearing this tunic. Also visible in the photograph is the stitching used to affix his Iron Cross 1st Class to the tunic (actually an Iron Cross 2nd Class with the jump ring removed as a wartime expedient), and the stitching holding the upper end of the medical device to the tunic sleeve. (C. Mason)

Left: Sanitäts-Unteroffizier Gerhard Volkmann of Fallschirm-Sturmgeschütz-Brigade 12 wearing his green assault gun wrapper in 1945. Volkmann joined the unit as a combat replacement after Normandy and kept his tunic and awards until 1996. (C. Mason)

A young Rifleman (Jäger) wearing an early flight blouse (Fliegerbluse) with a hand-sewn breast eagle. This photograph shows the less-than-uniform application of uniform regulations: The Waffenfarbe piping around his collar was abolished by an order published March 20, 1940, and the order requiring the wear of a breast eagle was not issued until November 1940. The tone of his collar tabs and collar piping, darker than the yellow of the flight branch or the copper of the signals branch, but lighter than the dark blue of the medical branch, suggests the continued use at this stage of the war of red piping for Flak-designated Fallschirmjäger units, such as the Fallschirm-Flak-MG battalion. (C. Mason)

Right: A studio portrait of a Fallschirmjäger veteran of the Russian Front at the rank of Unteroffizier Anwarter (NCO Candidate). He wears a non-regulation shirt and turtleneck for this portrait, along with his decorations and the squad leader's whistle and lanyard. Note that the rank gulls are affixed directly to the collar without collar tabs, and that he is wearing trousers with pocket flaps like paratrooper trousers, but without the openings at the knees. (C. Mason)

An unusual photo of a decorated Fallschirmjäger combat veteran who has left the paratroops and is now a member of the forestry service. (C. Mason)

Extremely small sized unissued example of a late-war flying blouse. The paper tag, still sewn to the tunic, indicates the maker and size. As this tunic was never issued, the metal gulls have not been added to the collar tabs, which are machine sewn. The breast eagle is machine zig-zag sewn. (Willi Zahn)

Troopers on Crete wearing (above) blue flying tunics, and (below) non-issue tunics (either custom made or captured).

The reverse of the Luftwaffe tropical tunic. This uniform was very popular with the troops. (C. Mason)

Typical Luftwaffe tropical tunic as worn by a Fallschirmjäger Major. Of interest are the rare Luftwaffe tropical equipment straps and Luftwaffe tropical officer's belt. (C. Mason)

A detail view of the tropical web gear and factory-applied breast eagle. (C. Mason)

Luftwaffe tropical tunic representing a Major in the Fallschirmtruppen. One noticeable difference between Luftwaffe tropical tunics and most other Wehrmacht tunics is the absence of collar tabs. This particular tunic was brought back by a U.S. veteran who served in both the Tunisian and Italian campaigns. (Willi Zahn)

Markings inside the left side of the tunic indicate the manufacturer and size. (Willi Zahn)

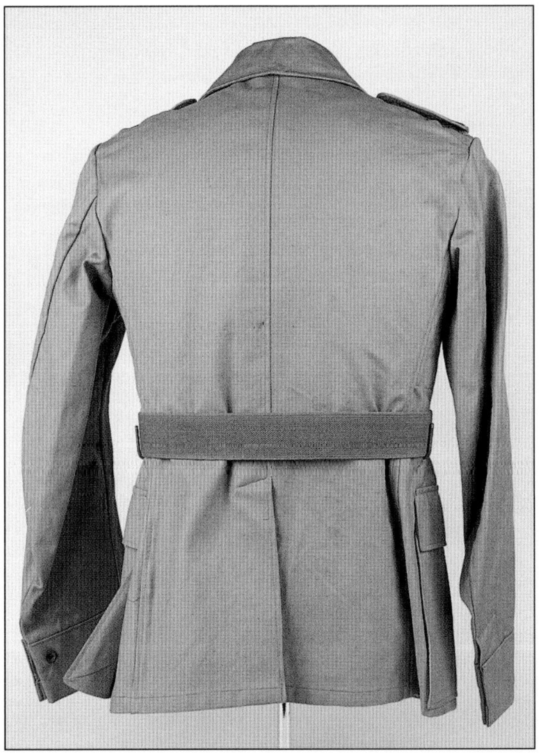

Rear view showing how the belt is supported by the belt hooks attached to the tunic. The small tan painted metal dish button can be seen on the left cuff. (Willi Zahn)

Unissued example of a tropical tunic in the rank of Feldwebel. The Luftwaffe tropical buckle is painted in an olive tan color and is dated 1942. Though tropical belts were available in various shades, this example is in a tan color often associated with Luftwaffe tropical items. (Willi Zahn)

As in most Luftwaffe uniforms items, the tropical breast eagle is machine applied. All the removable buttons on this tunic, including those for the shoulder boards, are painted in a tan color. (Willi Zahn)

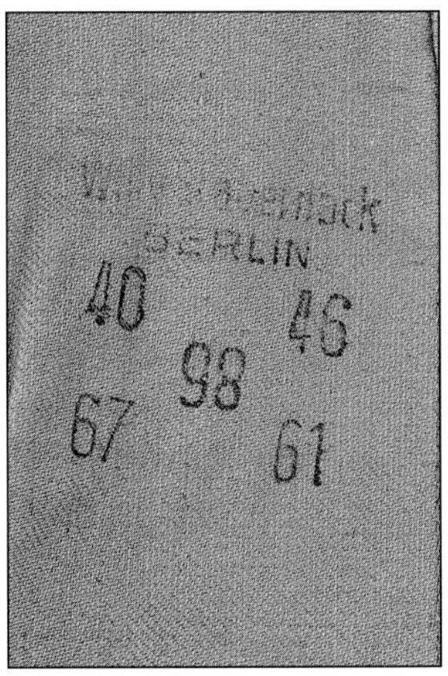

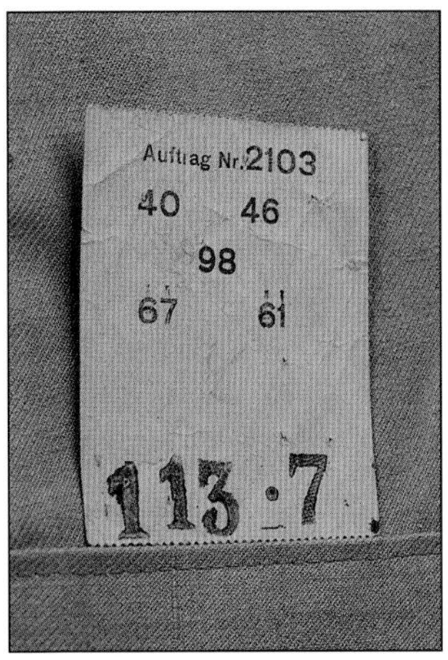

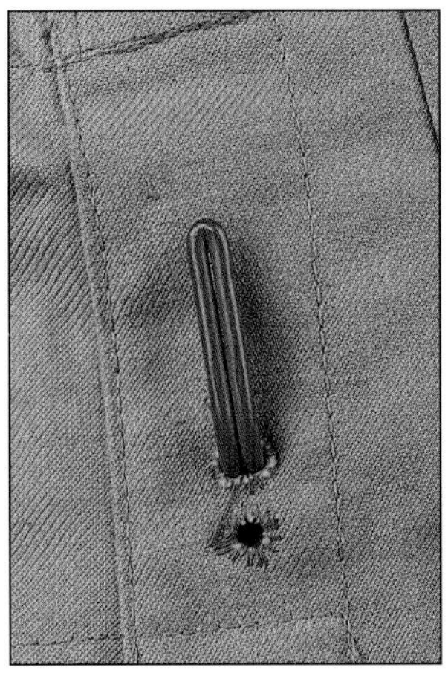

Right: The name of the manufacturer and the size markings present inside the left side of the tunic.
Right center: This paper issue tag was found inside one of the tunic pockets – the numbers match the size numbers stamped on the inside of the tunic. The tag was normally sewn to the left lower sleeve. The veteran who brought this tunic home carefully removed the tag and placed it, along with the thread that attached it, in an envelope and placed it in a pocket for safe keeping.
Far right: Left side view showing the tan painted belt hook and how it hooks into the tunic. (Willi Zahn)

Short sleeve Luftwaffe tropical shirt and a pair of Luftwaffe tropical shorts. The shorts have the same waist belt arrangement found on the long tropical trousers. The shirt has tan painted metal dish buttons for the front and pockets, and has tan painted tunic buttons for the shoulder boards. (Willi Zahn)

Rear view showing the construction of the tropical shorts with the two pockets and their hidden tan metal dish buttons. (Willi Zahn)

Markings found inside the shorts. The "LBA B 41" markings indicate that they are Luftwaffe issue, present at the Berlin depot and made in 1941. Though the fly uses tan metal dish buttons, the top two buttons are the standard Luftwaffe glass type. (Willi Zahn)

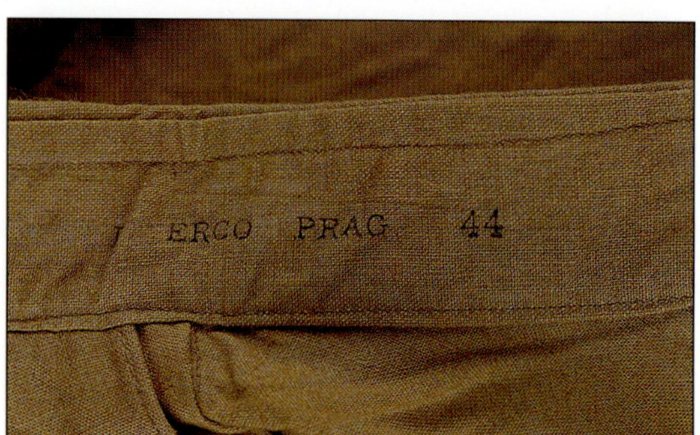

Markings found in the inside of the collar of the short sleeve shirt. (Willi Zahn)

Rear view of the late-war long sleeve shirt. The shirt is in a darker shade of fabric than most other Luftwaffe tropical clothing. (Willi Zahn)

Close-up of the breast eagle on the short sleeve shirt. Details of the pocket construction and tan metal dish button can be seen. (Willi Zahn)

Unusual variant of the Luftwaffe tropical long sleeve shirt. The shirt utilizes pressed paper buttons for the front, pockets and cuffs. An RB Nr code is stamped inside the collar. (Willi Zahn)

An early 1941 dated pair of Fallschirmjäger jump trousers. Early examples of these trousers seem to have a little more green color in the fabric than later examples. Like many other Luftwaffe clothing items, snaps are used to fasten pockets and the side seams of the leg. The snaps on these trousers are marked "Prym." (Willi Zahn)

Left: Rear view of the 1941 dated jump trousers showing details of the rear pockets, which have buttons. These trousers also have the "LBA" stamping, present on most Luftwaffe issue clothing. (Willi Zahn)

Right: Close up of the right side of the right leg displaying the flapped pocket for the Luftwaffe gravity knife. In front of the pocket is the hidden seam which has snaps and allows access to the leg required when removing the first pattern internal knee pads. Also shown is one of the side pull adjustment buckles and belt. (Willi Zahn)

A later 1943 dated pair of jump trousers. This pair is in a slightly darker color with more gray in it, common to many later war Wehrmacht uniforms. The markings consist of the date, RB Nr for the maker, a "LBA" stamp and size markings. (Willi Zahn)

Right: Rear view again showing the details of the pockets. Also visible is the left side waist adjustment belt. (Willi Zahn)

Left: This particular example uses a piece of earlier wool for the gravity knife pocket flap, showing the contrast between the two different shades. By observing the stitch lines of the gravity knife pocket one can get an idea of the size of the internal pocket. (Willi Zahn)

Left: Fallschirmjäger trousers with all snap closures of pockets and flaps. Right: The reverse of the Fallschirmjäger trousers. Of note are the snap closure on the left pocket (as seen) and the button closure on the right pocket. (C. Mason)

Detail of the gravity knife pocket built into the leg of the Fallschirmjäger trousers. (C. Mason)

Detail of the side and watch pockets. Of interest are the Prym snaps. Notice that much of the stitching is actually done with white thread. (C. Mason)

A close up of the markings inside a pair of Fallschirmjäger trousers. (C. Mason)

A detailed view of the leg opening on the Fallschirmjäger trousers. Of note are the "Prym" brand snaps, the only brand ever found on original trousers. Immediately after the war, the design was changed to read "Prym Original" on the female side, an inadvertent gift to collectors in future decades. (C. Mason)

This style of Fallschirmjäger trousers is identical to the previous pair, except that the side and watch pockets have button closures in place of snap closures. All other details are the same. (C. Mason)

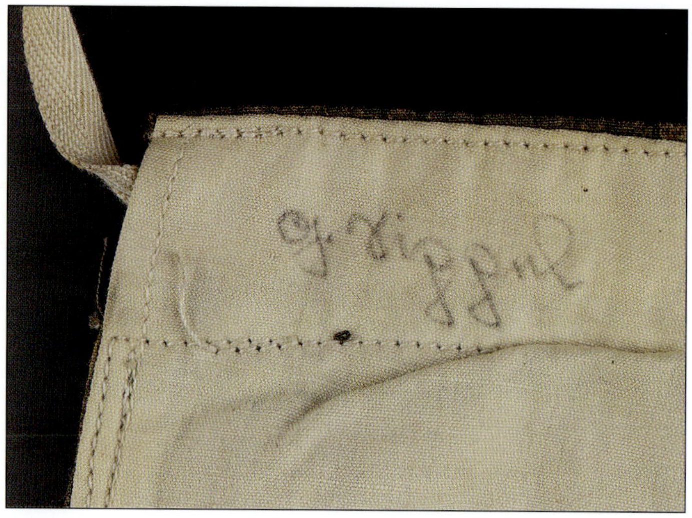

Detail view of the camouflage trousers belonging to Oberjäger Sippul. He has written his name in ink in both cuffs using the old Sutterlin script. (C. Mason)

Quilted reversible water pattern-to-white camouflage trousers which belonged to paratrooper Oberjäger Sippul. (C. Mason)

Chapter Two

Headgear

Helmets, Visor Hats, Caps

The single decal Fallschirmjäger helmet with early "spanner" bolts characterized by the small holes flanking the center ventilation hole. The two-pronged spanner used to tighten these bolts was rarely available in the field. (C. Mason)

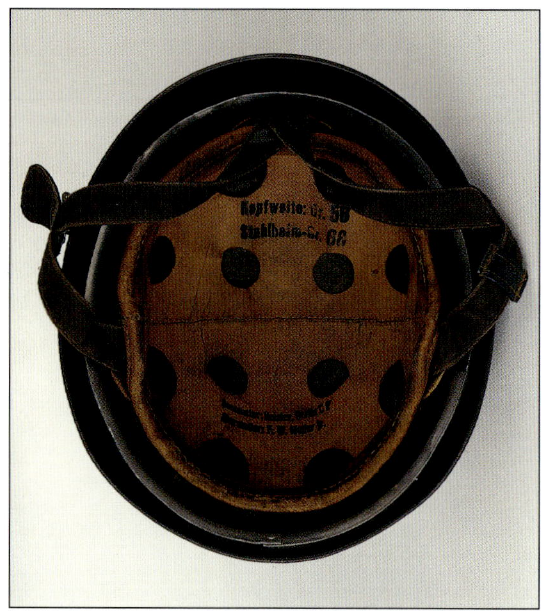

The inside of the single decal M38 Fallschirmjäger helmet showing liner details. (C. Mason)

Pre-war double decal M38 helmet. The helmet is finished in the early smooth apple green paint encountered on early double decal Heer M35 helmets. (Willi Zahn)

Right side view of the double decal M38 showing the national colors and another view of the apple green paint finish. (Willi Zahn)

Single decal M38 helmet with ventilated aluminum bolts in a rough dark green-gray paint finish. The ventilated slotted bolt was an improvement over the standard slotted aluminum bolt which did not allow for enough air to get into the helmet when worn tightly on the head. One common complaint among veterans of the Fallschirmtruppen was that the helmet was extremely hot, especially in the tropical regions of southern Europe. (Willi Zahn)

Example of an early M38 single decal spanner bolt helmet. This particular helmet is in a smooth dark green-gray paint finish and was brought home by a veteran of the 2nd Canadian Infantry Division who picked it up near Antwerp, Belgium in the fall of 1944. The recent introduction of near perfect helmets which are complete reproductions, require a detailed study of all the parts of original examples. (Willi Zahn)

Typical double decal M38 paratrooper helmet. Original double decal helmets are always found in this unique shade of pea green on both the inside and outside of the shell, and always have the early yellow rubber liner components. (C. Mason)

A typical example of the mid-to-late war M38 helmet with no decal and slotted aluminum bolts. (C. Mason)

The liner of this mid-war helmet still has the maker's name stamped on the leather rather than an RB Nr. (C. Mason)

Unissued late-war slotted aluminum M38 helmet.The decal is a green/gray subdued variation sometimes encountered on other Luftwaffe helmets. (Willi Zahn)

Interior view of the unissued helmet showing the marking of a late issue helmet. (Willi Zahn)

Another example of an unissued late-war M38, this time with no decal present. This helmet has the ventilated aluminum slotted bolts on the sides and steel slotted bolts on the rear. This particular bolt arrangement seems to be present on numerous examples of this exact style helmet. The paint appears to be more of a dark slate gray than the usual dark green-gray. (Willi Zahn)

Interior view of the dark slate gray no decal helmet. (Willi Zahn)

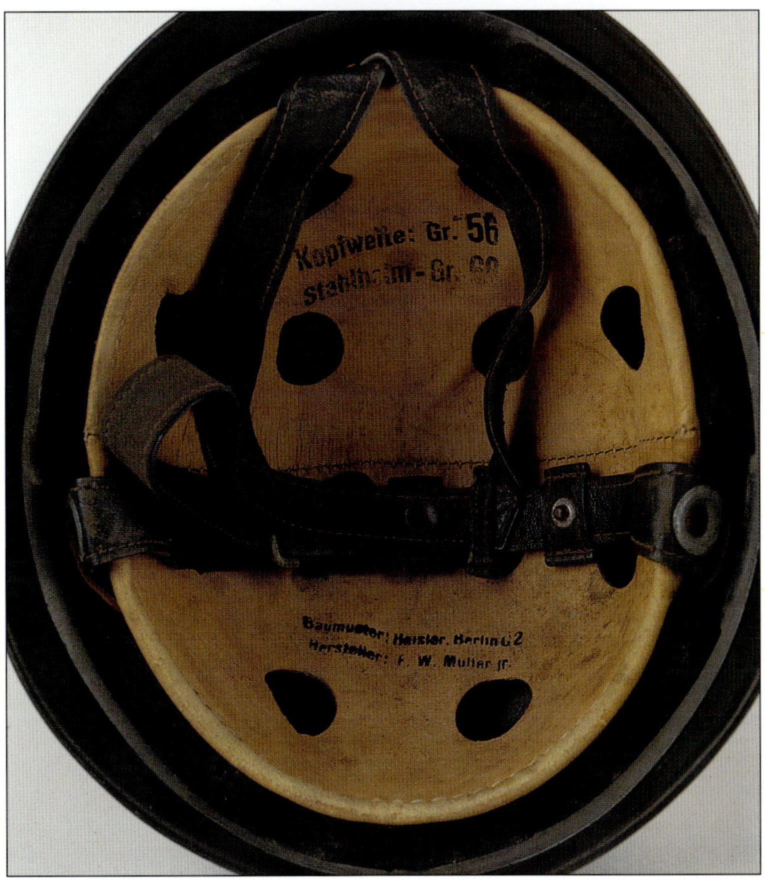

A rare very late war M38 Fallschirmjäger helmet in which standard helmet split pins have been used instead of bolts. Note that the final coat of paint was applied after the split pins were installed. This helmet has the last model chin straps. (C. Mason)

The liner of the late war paratrooper helmet. This helmet was apparently never issued. (C. Mason)

Fallschirmjäger helmet. This mint example is a later war style. The paint is a rough textured grey and the slotted bolts are made of polished aluminum. The Luftwaffe decal was never applied to this helmet. Later war examples can be found either with or without a decal. (Collection of Bill Shea, "The Ruptured Duck")

Liner and harness view clearly shows the liner size (Kopfweite: Gr) 58 and the shell size (Stahlhelm-Gr.) 68, as well as the manufacturer's name and address. The special paratrooper leather chinstrap harness had a soft chamois type leather on the interior and reduced friction where the harness would rub against the wearer's face.

Camouflage Fallschirmjäger helmet. Each camouflage helmet has its own distinctive look. This example was first sprayed with dark green paint then oversprayed with yellow paint. It features the earlier (first type) of spanner bolt. (Collection of Bill Shea, "The Ruptured Duck")

An example of sprayed camouflage paint on a single decal M38 paratrooper helmet in which the decal is still partially visible. These colors constitute what is often referred to as the "Normandy" camouflage scheme, for its frequent use in the summer of 1944 on the Normandy front. (C. Mason)

Helmet with a late-winter camouflage scheme of thick-textured reds and greens over a previous whitewashing. (C. Mason)

This photograph shows the inside of late winter camouflage scheme. The whitewashing included the inside of the rim, but the application of the later overpaint did not. (C. Mason)

An example of a very thick three-colored camouflage scheme in yellow, red and green paint mixed with sand and applied with a brush. (C. Mason)

This helmet was sent home by an American soldier from Tunisia. The pale sand tan and faint green of this camouflage scheme are classic north African colors. (C. Mason)

Another view of the Afrika Korps Fallschirmjäger helmet shows the pale green detail to advantage. (C. Mason)

A less common hand-painted example of a camouflage Fallschirmjäger helmet in Normandy colors. The olive green and mustard yellow were painted at the same time, creating a striking effect when the two colors ran together. This helmet, which apparently had additional baling wire affixed during the war, was found recently in Normandy. (C. Mason)

This spanner bolt M38 helmet has been camouflaged with a heavy sprayed coat of tan paint. While the paint was wet, fine gravel, sand and even some small pieces of wood have been rubbed into it. (Willi Zahn)

An example of a camouflage helmet that was brought home by a veteran of the 9th Infantry Regiment of the U.S. 2nd Infantry Division, who picked it up during the Normandy campaign. The helmet is named to an Oberfeldwebel, and has been sprayed with green and tan paint with sawdust rubbed into the paint while still wet. (Willi Zahn)

This particular helmet was brought home with a draw string splinter helmet cover still in place. The cover was only first removed when the helmet was purchased from the son of the veteran in 1996, thereby revealing the camouflage paint. (Willi Zahn)

A helmet with a unique brushed applied camouflage pattern in the colors of dark green, red brown and tan. The paratrooper who applied the pattern took care in painting around the eagle and by not applying a heavy coat of paint to the helmet bolts. (Willi Zahn)

Inside view of the brush stroke camouflaged helmet showing more details of the construction of the liner, chin straps, liner band and padding between the liner and the band. (Willi Zahn)

Right side view shows how this aspiring artist applied his brush strokes. Wartime photographs and numerous surviving examples indicate that the practice of camouflaging paratrooper helmets was quite common, especially in North Africa, Italy and in France during the Normandy campaign. (Willi Zahn)

Right side view of camouflaged chicken wire Fallschirmjäger helmet. A very distinctive helmet as it was first camouflaged in lighter greens and then the owner applied a "full basket" of chicken wire. This was a popular and easily accessible way for the soldiers to further mask their appearance. Leaves, branches and other types of foliage would be slipped in between the wire. (Collection of Bill Shea, "The Ruptured Duck")

Left side view. Note the worn camouflage paint which probably prompted the owner to use another camouflage option (the chicken wire). Also note the correct European style twist to the wire. This helmet features the first style spanner bolts.

Interior View. The markings are for the size of the liner (59) and the size of the shell (71). Paratrooper shells came in only three sizes: 66, 68 and 71. Liner sizes were available from 53 to 61.

Single decal Fallschirmjäger helmet with baling wire and chicken wire applied to retain camouflaging. The wear pattern of the wire on the paint is immediately evident. (C. Mason)

An interior view of the baling and chicken wire helmet shows how the two types of wire are affixed to the helmet rim. (C. Mason)

This unique M38 spanner bolt helmet is finished in a rough dark green-gray paint and has added several pieces of wire attached to it for the addition of camouflage. As original pictures prove, this exact style was seen during the Normandy campaign. (Willi Zahn)

Right: Wartime press release photo depicting Generalleutnant Schimpf, the commander of the 3rd Fallschirmjäger Division, and members of his staff during the Normandy invasion. Note the helmet on the paratrooper standing in the rear and how it compares to the original example of the helmet with wire shown above. (Willi Zahn)

These views show that the soldier who created this unique wire work had some talent and imagination. (Willi Zahn)

Another late-war single decal helmet that has had chicken wire attached to a piece of heavy bailing wire, which was then secured to the rim. This particular helmet was found in the attic of a house in Metz, France. The chicken wire has been galvanized to inhibit rust, which was commonly used by farmers during World War II. (Willi Zahn)

Opposite: The zinc coating on the chicken wire will still corrode over the years, as this example has. The corroding has been accelerated on the pieces that have been cut and have been tied into the bailing wire, which is not galvanized. In some areas the chicken wire that has been in contact with the bailing wire has completely rusted through. (Willi Zahn)

A typical example of equipment netting applied for holding foliage. This helmet was brought back by a U.S. veteran. (C. Mason)

The liner of the helmet with netting shows the method of holding the netting in place with cotton cording. (C. Mason)

The rare helmet net designed specifically for the paratrooper helmet, here displayed on a single decal helmet for illustration purposes. This net was made in very small quantities but has been identified in period photographs. (C. Mason)

Late-war single decal M38 with slotted aluminum bolts. The net is secured under the liner band and is further secured by four metal helmet net hooks, one of which is visible here. The chin strap on this helmet is a style encountered in the late-war period, and the leather is not of the usual high quality. (Willi Zahn)

This view shows another one of the metal hooks used to secure the net to the helmet. (Willi Zahn)

Late-war no decal M38 helmet. This example has had a net applied, though it is not original to the helmet – the net is standard Wehrmacht issue. The helmet is named to a Feldwebel in several places and is unit marked to a signal platoon of FJR12. The small piece of cord in the back is original to the helmet and was apparently used to secure the helmet to the soldier's field gear when not worn. (Willi Zahn)

Another example of the "Normandy" camouflage helmet combined with a bread bag strap for foliage. Notice the wear around the rim from the metal hook. (C. Mason)

A wonderful studio portrait of a Fallschirmjäger rifleman wearing the olive green jump smock, ordinary trousers and jackboots, and the Fallschirmjäger helmet with a bread bag affixed for camouflage. (C. Mason)

The splinter draw string helmet cover which was still attached to the camouflage saw dust helmet with the damage to the cover caused by the rim of the helmet. Original draw string covers are extremely rare and have been frequently reproduced over the years. (Willi Zahn)

Interior view of the helmet cover showing that the pattern is only printed on the outside – parts of the "rain" streaks have bled through. The faint purple ink is the manufacturer's stamp and size marking. (Willi Zahn)

This page and opposite: Various period examples of helmet camouflage.

Luftwaffe General Officer's Visor Cap. This handsome cap is made of blue wool and features a combination of celleon piping (around the crown and above and below the center band) and gold bullion eagle and wreath. This example is made by EREL (this particular model was called "PRIVAT"), (Collection of Bill Shea, "The Ruptured Duck")

Typical Luftwaffe officer's visor cap with a jaunty, partial "50-mission" look. (C. Mason)

A rarity, this is a Luftwaffe officer's "crusher." No regulations existed for this equivalent of the popular Army version, but several period photographs show such hats being worn by Fallschirmjäger officers. (C. Mason)

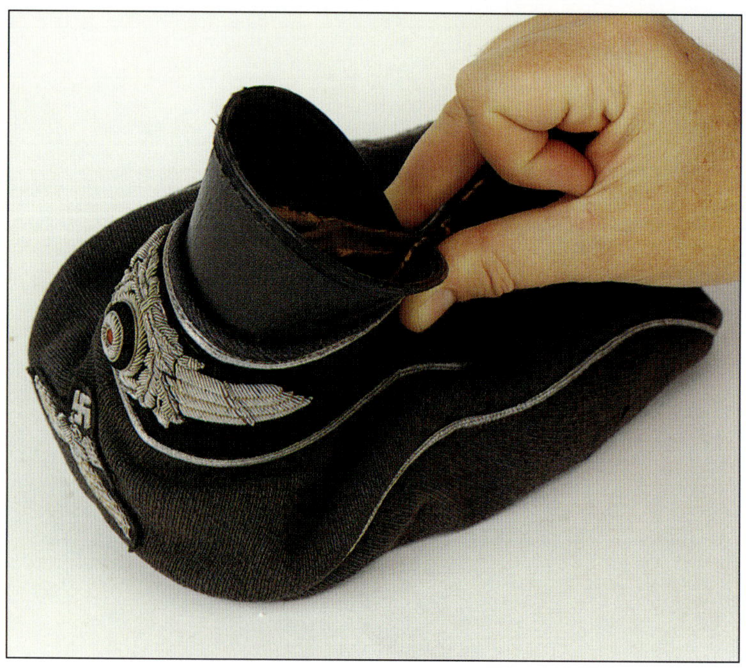

The non-regulation Luftwaffe crusher had a longer bill of soft leather like the regulation army officer's crusher, which could be folded in half without damage. This cap never had chin cords. (C. Mason)

Luftwaffe officer's summer visor, in this case a double-Erel marked model with vented Kokarde. (C. Mason)

Luftwaffe Summer Officer's Visor Cap. This cap was used by all branches of the Luftwaffe. The white top is removable for cleaning purposes as is the silver bullion white backed eagle. The silver bullion piping also distinguishes this as an officer's cap. Most of these were private purchase. (Collection of Bill Shea, "The Ruptured Duck")

Luftwaffe enlisted man's visor cap for flight and paratroop personnel issued to a Fallschirmjäger. (C. Mason)

Right: Reverse of the leather sweatband has the issue stamp of the 3rd Battalion, Fallschirmjäger Regiment I in the correct format and nomenclature. (C. Mason)

Luftwaffe enlisted man's summer visor with white top and yellow Waffenfarbe piping for flight personnel and Fallschirmjäger. (C. Mason)

Pre-war enlisted service cap which is unit marked to the 1st FJR, a practice only done in the pre-war years. (Willi Zahn)

Right: Interior markings showing that the cap was manufactured in 1939, sized 58 and made by a Berlin firm. (Willi Zahn)

Below: Unit markings stamped to the inside of the leather sweatband. The markings of "Stab II/Fallschirm-Jäger Rgt 1" indicate that it was issued to a member of the staff of the second battalion. The second battalion was raised from members of the Heer's Fallschirm Infanterie Bataillon, which was absorbed into the Luftwaffe in 1939. (Willi Zahn)

Right: Luftwaffe M43 Field Cap. This field cap was standard issue to all Luftwaffe troops (M43 is short for the Model 1943). This cap is made of a wool material and has a one button closure on the front of the flap. The one button style is of later production and was still another move to economize production. (Collection of Bill Shea, "The Ruptured Duck")

Luftwaffe M43 Field Cap. This cap is made of wool material and has a two button (earlier version) closure on the front of the flap. These flaps could be pulled down over the ears in cold weather. The insignia (eagle and cockade) are machine embroidered. (Collection of Bill Shea, "The Ruptured Duck")

The Luftwaffe Bergmütze, or mountain cap, is characterized by its stubby brim and a higher front crown than the typical M43 cap. Below: The Bergmütze is also typically found with a leather half-sweatband as seen here in this interior view. (C. Mason)

A true Luftwaffe officer's M43 cap. It differs from the enlisted version by the addition of silver piping around the crown and silver wire Luftwaffe eagle. (C. Mason)

Right: Interior of the Luftwaffe officer's M43 cap shows the leather half-sweatband and a dark blue lining very similar to the lining used in the splinter-pattern M43 cap shown on page 104. (C. Mason)

Officer at right center wears a mountain cap with added Luftwaffe insignia. Crete May, 1941.

A 1942 dated single button field cap. These caps were eventually replaced by the M43 cap, but were observed in use until the end of the war. (Willi Zahn)

Right: Inside markings of the single button field cap. Note the leather sweatband and the well-made lining. (Willi Zahn)

None of these caps was ever produced in a factory, and any cap of this type with any industrial markings such as a size stamp, RB Nr code or maker marking is a reproduction. The side view shows simple holes punched for ventilation over the ears. The availability of grommets and grommet setters in operational theaters where such caps were made was minimal. (C. Mason)

A field-made M43 style cap manufactured from splinter-pattern Zeltbahn material with a Luftwaffe eagle hand sewn to the front. This cap was found in a German home near Cologne by an estate sale agent in the 1980's and has since been analyzed and dated by a textile forensics expert. (C. Mason)

While any field-made cap of this style is suspect, this cap has a number of features consistent with quality field work of the period. The lining, for example, has been removed from another cap and reused here. The stitching marks where the original diamond shield was affixed are still evident. (C. Mason)

Luftwaffe Officer's Overseas Cap. This cap is made of blue wool with a distinctive silver bullion piping around the scallops of the cap. The machine embroidered eagle and cockade are the same as those encountered on the "other ranks" cap (a bullion eagle would tend to get damaged (split) as the cap was so flat). (Collection of Bill Shea, "The Ruptured Duck")

Factory-made Luftwaffe officer's continental overseas cap with silver piping and officer's silver wire insignia. Improvised versions made by adding silver wire to an enlisted cap are more common than the true officer's model of this cap. (C. Mason)

Standard issue Luftwaffe enlisted overseas cap dated 1941. (Willi Zahn)

Interior markings of the continental overseas cap. Earlier caps like this one are lined in a cotton material, while later issue caps were lined in the rayon style lining. (Willi Zahn)

A later issue enlisted overseas cap. As the war progressed the quality of the wool used to manufacture clothing began to deteriorate, and the items took on a different shade of blue-gray. (Willi Zahn)

An example of a 1942 dated tropical overseas cap in blue-gray cotton. Both the eagle and the cockade are on a standard wool backing. Luftwaffe tropical uniforms in blue/gray cotton are extremely uncommon, and do not seem to be dated beyond 1942. (Willi Zahn)

Inside markings of the 1942 dated blue-gray tropical hat. The maker is Berolina, a common maker of Luftwaffe tropical overseas caps. The "59" indicates size. (Willi Zahn)

The later style of Luftwaffe tropical visor cap with all BeVo insignia. The chin strap has been reversed for aesthetic reasons, as is commonly seen in wartime photographs. The actual front side of the leather chin strap is black leather with a distinctive diamond crosshatch pattern. (C. Mason)

The early style of Luftwaffe tropical visor cap with a tri-color Stumpfwerk pip on tan cotton and a machine-sewn tropical breast eagle as constructed at the factory. This cap was referred to in jest by the troops as a "Hermann Meyer" cap, a sarcastic reference to Hermann Göring's pre-war boast that if a single enemy bomb ever fell on Germany, "you can call me Hermann Meyer." This cap is complete with havelock and issue chin strap, which has been reversed. (C. Mason)

Two Fallschirmjäger and a civilian in North Africa in 1943. The man on the left is wearing his paratrooper badge and the "Herman Meyer" cap, which was not popular with the Fallschirmjäger. He is carrying his paratrooper helmet in his right hand. (C. Mason)

The officer at left in this tropical scene wears a Meyer cap with added officer chincords, a common practice. Soldier at center wears a captured British helmet net.

Rare Luftwaffe officer's factory-made M41 tropical cap. (C. Mason)

Right: A view of the back of the Luftwaffe officer's M41 tropical cap. (C. Mason)

Factory-made, issue Luftwaffe tropical M41 cap. Because of the scarcity of these caps at the time and their popularity with the troops, many locally-made improvisations of this cap exist. The insignia on the front of this cap is typical of the factory-made issue cap. (C. Mason)

Right: Factory-produced caps had only a light linen lining and a full leather sweatband, which in this cap has rotted away, leaving only the rim still under the stitching which held in it place. (C. Mason)

Luftwaffe tropical M41 hat. This particular piece is a field-made version as commonly used in North Africa and Italy. (Willi Zahn)

Rear view of the factory made Luftwaffe tropical M41 cap. (C. Mason)

Luftwaffe Tropical Field Cap. Very salty example of a field-made piece of headgear. This was not uncommon whenever access to factory-produced equipment was not possible. This distinctive hat is made of tan cloth material and utilized a Luftwaffe breast eagle instead of a small field cap eagle. The cockade is machine embroidered. (Collection of Bill Shea, "The Ruptured Duck")

The factory-made Luftwaffe officer's tropical overseas cap is rare. This one was manufactured by the firm of Berolina in Berlin in 1941. Below: The interior of the Luftwaffe tropical officer's overseas cap shows the maker markings. (C. Mason)

A typical field expedient was the addition of silver piping to an enlisted man's tropical overseas cap to create an officer's cap. (C. Mason)

An unusual field improvisation, a Luftwaffe tropical overseas cap modeled on the army pattern, with a tropical tunic eagle and tropical pip scrounged as insignia. (C. Mason)

Luftwaffe enlisted tropical overseas cap dated 1942 and made by the Berlin firm of Berolina. (Willi Zahn)

Interior markings of the tropical overseas cap. The lining is made from a different fabric than the outer shell. (Willi Zahn)

Another example of an enlisted tropical overseas cap dated 1941 and made by the Berlin firm of G.A. Hoffmann. This variation is made out of a much thinner cotton fabric than the previous cap. (Willi Zahn)

Right above: Tropical Luftwaffe pith helmet was issued to troops in North Africa, but was not popular with them. This example is dated 1942. As is the standard for most Luftwaffe tropical items, the color is more tan than Heer or Kriegesmarine tropical uniform items. (Willi Zahn)

Right: Right side view of the tropical pith helmet displaying the national colors. Like Heer pith helmets, the emblems were attached by inserting the prongs of the emblem through the pith helmet and bending them over on the inside. (Willi Zahn)

Right: The officer at left wears a captured Dutch pith helmet in this scene from Crete.

Chapter Three

Insignia and Badges, Cuff Titles

Above: The obverse of the Fallschirmschützenabzeichen produced by the firm of Wilhelm Deumer in Lüdenscheid. The Deumer badge is undoubtedly the highest quality paratrooper badge produced by the Third Reich. It is an unusually heavy badge with striking detail. (C. Mason)

Above right: The reverse of the Deumer badge. The quality of construction is evident in the wide hinge assembly, the attention to detail in the finish of the rivets, and the clasp. This badge is hand inscribed with the date of the owner's parachute badge award, "9 Novb 1940." (C. Mason)

Right: One of several variations encountered of the award case for the Fallschirmschützenabzeichen. This variation omits the word "Abzeichen." (C. Mason)

Above: The Fallschirmschützenabzeichen produced by the firm of Berg & Nolte in Lüdenscheid. Their trademark marking is seen here, "B&N L." Berg & Nolte were prolific manufacturers of award badges during the Third Reich. Their paratrooper badge is of average quality. (C. Mason)

Above right: The reverse of the Berg & Nolte badge. The original owner has scratched his initials into the wreath, "W H," a common practice. The reason for the unique departure from the traditional blue lining is probably accident or temporary material shortage. (C. Mason)

Right: Another variation of the badge case. This case is highly unusual in that it is lined in red rather than blue. (C. Mason)

Above: The Fallschirmschützenabzeichen produced by the firm of GH Osang in Dresden. This maker has been reproduced after the war, but the quality of the original badge is evident here and in the reverse view. (C. Mason)

Above right: As is evident here, the original GH Osang paratrooper badge was a high quality piece. Although the hinge is narrower than the Imme & Sohn or the Deumer badges, the rivets and clasp are well finished. One characteristic of the GH Osang badge which differs from other makers is the pin, which is rectangular rather than round in cross-section. (C. Mason)

Right: This badge case is flatter and squarer than most, with an embossed border line. (C. Mason)

Above: The Pleuger & Voss is perhaps the rarest of the Fallschirmschützen-abzeichenen. The quality of materials is equal to the Deumer badge, and the workmanship is excellent. In comparison to other makers, however, it is almost delicate, being markedly both smaller and lighter than the Deumer. The pin design is unique among paratrooper badges. (C. Mason)

Above right: The quality of the diminutive Pleuger & Voss badge is evident here, as is the unique pin. (C. Mason)

Right: One of the most commonly found cases for the paratrooper badge is this style used by the firm of Pleuger & Voss of Lüdenscheid. (C. Mason)

Above: The Fallschirmschützenabzeichen produced by the firm of Imme & Sohn was a very high quality badge, although the quality of the metals is not as good as that used in the Deumer and Pleuger & Voss badges. The wreath is more elongated in this design. (C. Mason)

Above right: The reverse of the Imme & Sohn badge shows the superb quality workmanship that went into the construction of this badge. The wide pin hinge, superior finishing on the rivets and the design of the clasp are all evidence of an outstanding craftsman. (C. Mason)

Right: Still another variation of the paratrooper badge case. (C. Mason)

Above and above right: This late-war badge is marked "GWL" identifying the maker as Gebrüder Wegerhoff in Lüdenscheid. (Willi Zahn)

Right: A case for the jump badge in metal. Note the deep blue color of the box, a shade that is absent on the numerous reproductions. (Willi Zahn)

Above: The declining quality resulting from wartime conditions is evident here in this unissued badge made by the firm of F.W. Assman & Sohn of Lüdenscheid. The eagle and wreath are constructed of the same metal, with an inexpensive wash gilting applied to the eagle (as was done with original Close Combat Clasps in Gold, for example), an indication of production in late 1944 or 1945. (C. Mason)

Above right: The reverse of the Assman badge shows the reverse of the eagle was not gilt washed. The badge still shows an effort at good craftsmanship under the circumstances, although an inferior hinge assembly was dictated by the materials available. The marking, with the stylized "A" and the "L64" (a number assigned by the Leistungsgemeinschaft deutscher Ordenshersteller, or LDO) is typical of Assmann products. Also unique to original Assmann badges is the tiny numeral above the right rivet. Both "1" and "2" have been observed, possibly die numbers. (C. Mason)

Right: This case is closer to black in color than the midnight blue found in most badge cases. (C. Mason)

Left: By war's end, Germany industry was strained to the breaking point by material shortages and the collapse of the transportation system. Hinged cases for awards gave way to simpler expedients, such as this cardboard box for the Fallschirmschützenabzeichen. (C. Mason)

The wear of the Fallschirmschützenabzeichen was not confined to the Luftwaffe. This very rare photograph depicts an Army officer veteran of Narvik (right) wearing the Luftwaffe paratrooper badge. A very small number of army soldiers were dropped into Norway on an emergency basis without prior parachute training and were awarded the badge. Men of the Brandenburg Regiment who became parachute qualified before 1944, when the Army badge was reintroduced, also received and wore the Luftwaffe version of the badge. (C. Mason)

Two Fallschirmschützenabzeichenen in cloth. On the left is a private purchase example created on a higher quality wool backing than found on issue examples. On the right, the most common pattern of the padded badge. An oval of soft cloth padding was placed between the badge front and the backing material to give a raised profile. (C. Mason)

Above and below: At left, an example of the unpadded issue Fallschirmschützenabzeichen in cloth. On the right, a variation of the padded cloth badge with a subdued wreath. (C. Mason)

Right: An Oberjäger (Corporal) wears the Fallschirmschützenabzeichen in cloth. He is also wearing a wound badge and the ribbon for the Iron Cross 2nd Class sewn to his lapel in the correct position. (C. Mason)

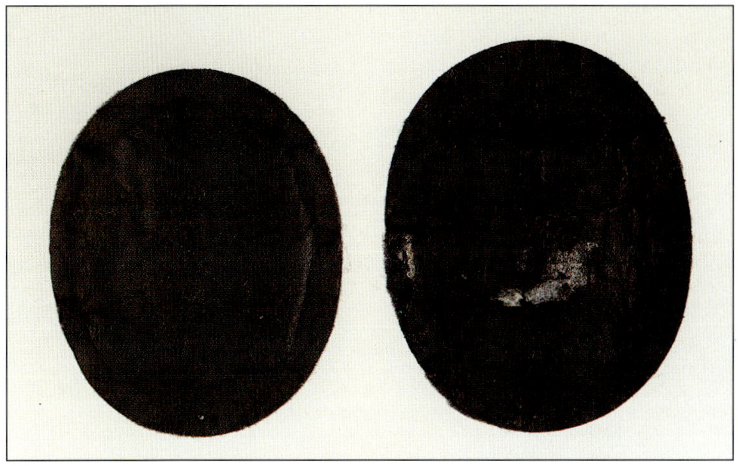

Another variation of the padded cloth paratrooper badge, with a brighter yellow used for the eagle but without the subdued wreath. (C. Mason)

Two very rare variants of the cloth version of the Fallschirmschützenabzeichen. At left, the army version of the badge on feldgrau wool. On the right, a green-backed example for wear on the assault gun tunic by members of Fallschirm-Sturmgeschütz-Brigaden 11 and 12. (C. Mason)

Two examples of the Fallschirmschützenabzeichen in cloth awarded for the completion of six jumps. These cloth jump badges were commonly worn by enlisted members of the Fallschirmtruppen on their flying blouse. (Willi Zahn)

A cloth officer's version of the Fallschirmschützenabzeichen.

The cloth version of the Fallschirmschützenabzeichen was produced by embroidering over an Unterlagen, or underlay pattern. The pattern was die cut from card stock. (C. Mason)

Left: This is a single rivet example of the Ground Combat Badge – a good quality construction for this award. Right: The original owner has scratched his name into the reverse side of the badge. The single rivet attachment point for the eagle is visible, as is the brass pin and barrel hinge assembly. (C. Mason)

Left: Some of the highest quality Ground Combat Badges were produced by the firm of G H Osang in Dresden. This is a well-detailed badge made from good quality materials. Right: The reverse of the G H Osang badge shows the wide pin and three rivet construction. The pin clasp is the same style of catch as the firm used on their paratrooper badge. (C. Mason)

The Luftwaffe Ground Combat Badge also came in a cardboard box towards the end of the war. There are as many different makers of this badge as there are of the paratrooper badge, but it is rarely of the same quality and is often found without any markings at all. (C. Mason)

Left: The Ground Combat Badge was also produced in a cloth version. This one is done in silver bullion and black thread on a gray wool background. Right: Reproductions of this badge are close to the original, but the backing is the giveaway. The kind of paper backing seen here has proven difficult to replicate. (C. Mason)

Left: A cloth version of the Luftwaffe Glider Pilot's badge. Glider pilots wore Fallschirmjäger equipment and fought as infantry upon landing. There is some damage to the wool underneath the eagle's beak on this example. The cloth version is rare. Right: The reverse of the cloth version of the Glider Pilot's badge. (C. Mason)

Left: Examples of Luftwaffe uniform eagles. The three on the right are the type found on tropical shirts, while the top two on the left are found on tropical tunics. On the lower left is an example of the eagle found on the light blue uniform shirt – this example has never been sewn on. Right: Rear view of the eagles showing that one is still stitched to a piece of tropical tunic. It was common for veterans to cut these eagles off as souvenirs, and many still include part of the uniform it was sewn to. (Willi Zahn)

Left: Examples of Luftwaffe paratrooper smock eagles. The three on the right are the type found on early second model green step-in smocks, thought they are also sometimes encountered on splinter smocks. The two on the lower left are splinter backed eagles which are found on early second model and third model splinter smocks. The eagle on the upper left is the camouflage type sometimes encountered on late-war third model tan and water pattern smocks. Right: Rear views of the smock eagles. Note that the one on the upper left is still sewn to a piece of water pattern smock material. (Willi Zahn)

Left: Examples of late-war eagles on a thin cotton twill backing. These types of eagles are found on various Luftwaffe clothing, including late-war jump smocks. Right: Rear view of the eagles on a thin cotton twill backing. The backs show details which are only present on original eagles, something which the numerous reproductions fail to have. (Willi Zahn)

Left: These eagles are sewn onto a HBT backing in various shades. Though not encountered on paratrooper smocks, these eagles can be found on Luftwaffe ground division jackets and HBT tunics. Right: Rear view showing the detail of the machine sewn eagles. (Willi Zahn)

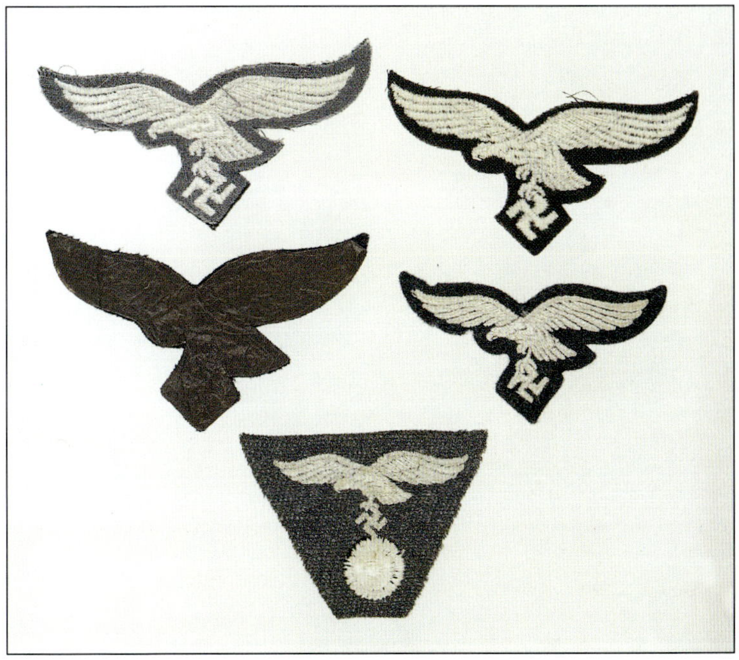

Several examples of wool backed eagles found on tunics and headgear. (Willi Zahn)

An example of a true paratroop smock rank device on flecked olive green backing, in this case for an Oberjäger. Use of rank devices designed for flight suits on other backings was widespread, but this is the only version designed specifically for the jump smock. (C. Mason)

Two examples of Luftwaffe helmet decals, the style worn on paratrooper helmets. The top decal shows the rear view, the side which goes against the helmet. The bottom decal shows how the paper protects the front side of the decal. The Germans applied these decals in a meticulous manner, unlike the technique and type of decals applied to models today. Proof of how well they have been applied is demonstrated by the fact that most helmets are already between fifty-five and sixty years old. (Willi Zahn)

Left: The pointed arms of the Iron Cross 1st Class snagged easily in clothing and equipment. Although against regulations, period photographs do show some use of cloth versions of the Iron Cross on combat uniforms. Seen here are the obverses of two approaches to the problem, the all-cloth and bullion version below, and a unique octagonal cloth version in which a black velvet interior is bordered by the front portion of the Iron Cross frame, above. Right: The reverses of the cloth versions. The prongs holding the metal half-frame to the backing are visible under the paper on the badge above. Both of these styles are very rare. (C. Mason)

Left: The Iron Cross 1st Class awarded to Leutnant Wilhelm Reinhardt, Kompanie Chef, 9. Kompanie, Fallschirmjäger Regiment 1 in Italy. Right: The reverse of Leutnant Reinhardt's Iron Cross shows his name and unit scratched into the silver: "III/1" on the top line for III. Bataillon, Fallschirmjäger Regiment 1, his name on the second line, and "9.Kp" for the 9th Company on the bottom. (C. Mason)

Three Fallschirmjäger cufftitles, from top to bottom, Fallschirmjäger Regiment 2 enlisted personnel, Fallschirm Division non-commissioned officers, Fallschirm Division enlisted personnel. (C. Mason)

Cufftitles for Fallschirmjäger Regiment 1 non-commissioned officers, top, enlisted personnel, center, and a Fallschirmjäger Regiment 1 NCO cufftitle which has had the numeral "1" removed, possibly done as a keepsake for a man in another regiment. (C. Mason)

A close up view of the Fallschirmjäger Regiment 1 NCO cufftitle. Of interest is the extremely high quality hand embroidery which has created this piece. (C. Mason)

Above: The Kreta cufftitle was awarded to all military personnel who landed on the island by air or sea between May 20 and May 27. Pilots and navy personnel in the vicinity were also eligible. This specimen has an RB Nr code stamp on the back. Also note the single strand of yellow thread running through the bottom edge on the reverse. (C. Mason)

Right: This Fallschirmjäger Oberfeldwebel displays his new Kreta cufftitle in 1943. (C. Mason)

Right: An example of the lapel pin on its original LDO sales card for serving Fallschirmjäger on leave in civilian clothing, or former Fallschirmjäger released from active duty as a result of wounds or injuries. (C. Mason)

Left: Before the falling star, or comet (Komet) became standardized as a tactical marking for the famed Sturm Regiment, the device of a diving eagle clutching a bomb was used as a unit symbol. This unofficial enameled stick-pin is typical of Luftwaffe unit stickpins sometimes worn on the Fliegerbluse by flight personnel, a practice proscribed by regulations but often tolerated by unit commanders as a morale builder. (C. Mason)

Far left: This very rare period book by Walter Gericke, Commander of the IV. Bataillon of the Sturm Regiment, is titled "From Maleme to Chania, Battle and Victory of the Sturm Regiment." The cover depicts the early diving eagle of the Sturm Regiment, which apparently preceded the Komet as a symbol of the unit. (C. Mason)

Left: The rare unit distinctive of the II. Fallschirm Korps, known as the "Meindl Badge" to collectors. The badge incorporates the initial "M" of the Korps commander, General Eugen Meindl, with a winged fist inside a rope border. (C. Mason)

Below: General Gustav Wilke awarding the Iron Cross to men of the 5. Fallschirm Division in France. He is wearing the distinctive of the II. Fallschirm Korps, known to collectors as the "Meindl Badge," on the side of his M43 cap. (C. Mason)

A locally-made pin-back Komet worn by a Crete veteran of the Sturm Regiment. The Komet device was used as a tactical symbol on vehicles and flags. There is also evidence of some use of the symbol as a personal device, including a photograph of this type of pin being worn by a Sturm Regiment officer on his M43 cap in Italy. (C. Mason)

Right: The unit pinback distinctive of the 3. Fallschirm Division commanded by General Schimpf. The device, created by a member of the division in a design competition, incorporates the initial "S" for its divisional commander and the numeral "3" in the stylized format of a paratrooper badge. (C. Mason)

Right: The unit distinctive of the I. Fallschirm Korps in Italy, in the form of a stylized parachute in red, black and white enamel, worn as a cap device on the M43 cap. The design was the unit's tactical symbol. (C. Mason)

Far right: This pocket-sized guide for rear-area security against saboteurs and partisans was produced by the I. Fallschirm-Korps in Italy. It is entitled, "Safe is Sure – Behind the Front, Too." The red, white and black parachute symbol of the I. Fallschirm-Korps appears in the upper left hand corner. (C. Mason)

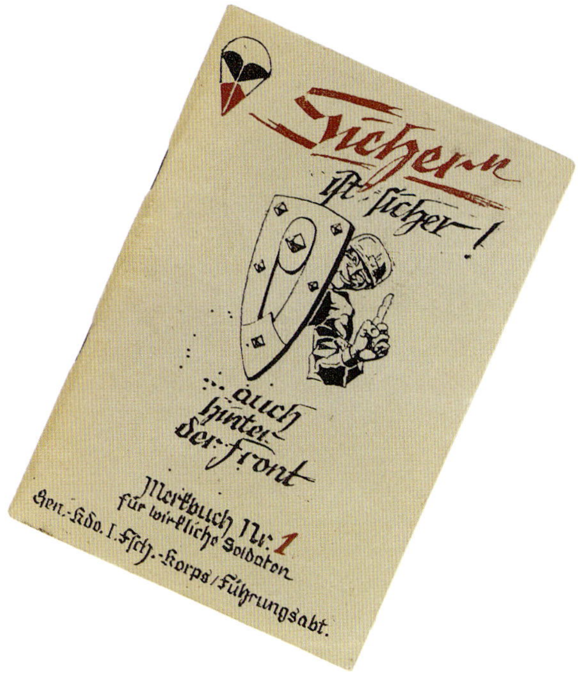

Below: In this photograph taken in Italy, a very tired Field Marshall Albert Kesselring (right) wears the I. Fallschirm Korps device on the side of his M43 cap. Notice the crossed Field Marshall batons on his shoulderboards. (C. Mason)

Examples of rings worn by Fallschirmjäger. On the left, two examples of the most popular design sold in garrison towns. On the right, examples of two campaign commemoratives, for Brest and Kreta. The Brest ring is fashioned from low quality metal and was probably made in a POW camp. (C. Mason)

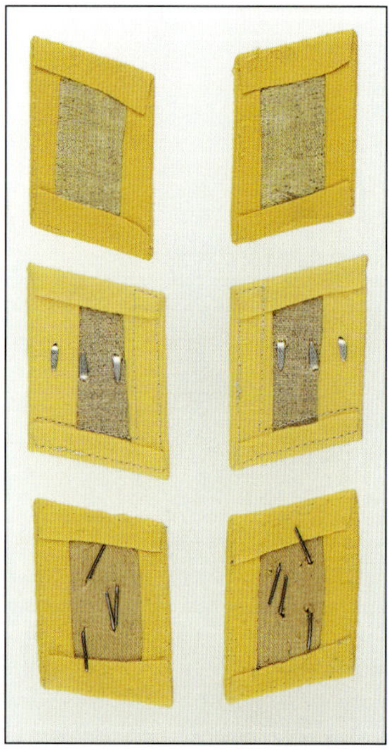

Left: Several sets of Luftwaffe collar tabs. The golden yellow branch color represents both the flying branch and paratrooper arm of the Luftwaffe. The top set have not had any rank applied, the middle set is for an Unteroffizer and represent a style of collar tab used on the great coat, and the bottom set is for the rank of Gefreiter. Right: Rear view showing details of the construction, backing and applied rank gulls. (Willi Zahn)

Two pair of Luftwaffe shoulder boards in HBT material. These boards are typically encountered on both the green and blue/gray versions of the Luftwaffe HBT tunics, though they are also sometimes worn on ground division camouflage smocks. (Willi Zahn)

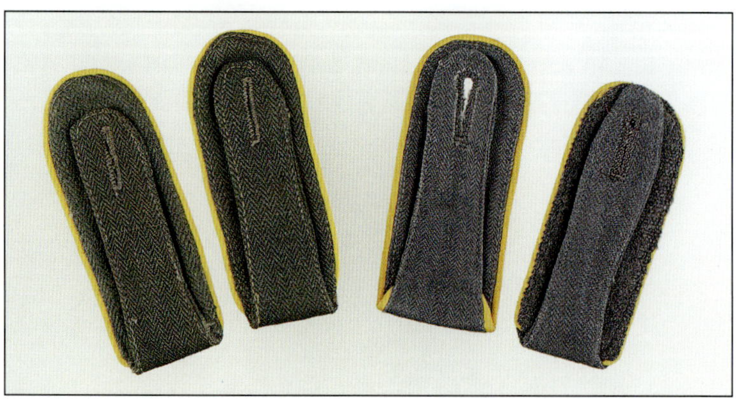

Two pair of Luftwaffe tropical shoulder boards in tan cotton material. The top set represents the rank of Feldwebel, while the bottom set represents the enlisted ranks. The back view shows the details of the tongue and button holes. (Willi Zahn)

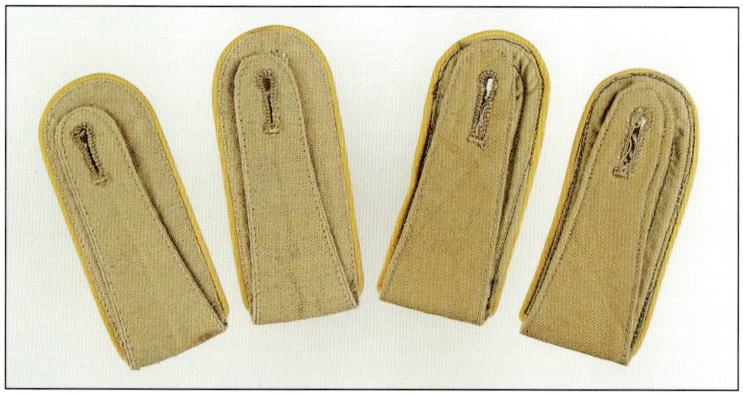

Once again two pair of Luftwaffe shoulder boards, these being the standard blue/gray wool variety common to most Luftwaffe flying blouses and service tunics. The top pair represents the rank of Unteroffizer, commonly referred to as Oberjäger in the Fallschirmtruppen. The bottom pair represents the enlisted ranks. (Willi Zahn)

Chapter Four

Equipment

A pair of front lace second model jump boots. The second model boots were introduced in the beginning of 1941 and were intended to replace the first model side lace boots. (Willi Zahn)

Rear and side view of the same pair. Note the original soles and heels which used nails that were flush with the sole to prevent the paratrooper from tripping inside the aircraft. These soles and heels quickly wore out and most surviving examples have been resoled either during or after the war. Recent examples of extremely well-made reproduction front lace boots coming out of Europe, take advantage of the fact that there was no standard way of resoling them. (Willi Zahn)

An unissued pair of mid-war, front-lacing Fallschirmjäger boots in cordovan leather. After the side-lacing pattern was abandoned, the first front-lacing boots continued to be made with rubber soles, before wartime shortages of rubber forced a switch to leather. Front-lace Fallschirmjäger boots always have twelve pairs of lacing eyelets. (C. Mason)

Detail of the upper of the front lace boots shows the characteristic embossed markings in the leather. (C. Mason)

Another characteristic of German jump boots is seen here in this detail of the boot heel. The concave groove running all the way around the heel is believed to be for ski bindings. (C. Mason)

Opposite: This photo taken in Crete shows both the early side lace, and second model front lace boots in use.

Issued and worn pair of Fallschirmjäger boots in brown leather. Three of the wooden pins securing the sole to the boot have worked their way loose. (C. Mason)

This pair of officer's riding boots was worn by Fallschirmjäger Stabsarzt Dr. Karl Semm of the Fallschirm-Aufklärungs-Abteilung 12 instead of the issue jump boots throughout the Normandy campaign in 1944. Period photographs indicate paratroop officers sometimes preferred the stylish and characteristic riding boots over jump boots. (C. Mason)

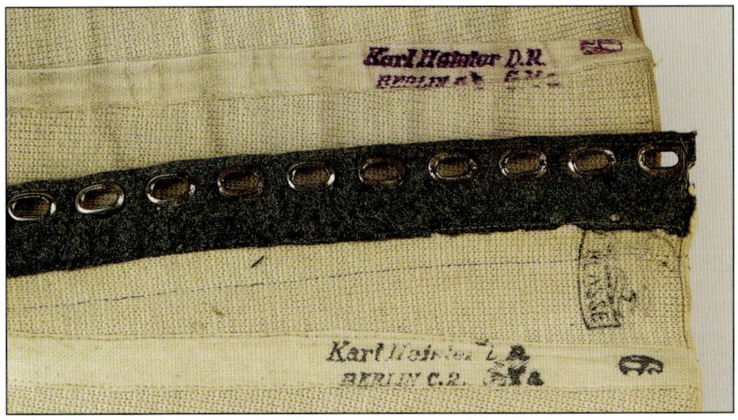

Left: Two examples of pre-war internal knee pads. These pads were worn under the jump trousers and were in use before the external style became available in 1940. These pads were designed to be removed by opening the lateral slash on the outside of each leg on the jump trousers and pulling the leather lace which bound the pad together. The difficulty in removing these pads was one of the reasons there were replaced by the external style. Right: The name of the manufacturer is clear in this photos along with the "6" and "9" which represents the size of this mismatched set. (Willi Zahn)

Typical pair of protective kneepads. Note the RB Nr code on the inside of the pad on the right. (C. Mason)

A well-worn pair of protective kneepads showing a repair done at one of the jump schools with green canvas. The damage to these pads is a good illustration of why they were part of the standard jump equipment. The RZ parachutes deployed in half the vertical height of the U.S. T-series parachutes, permitting lower drop altitudes and reducing exposure to ground fire, but they practically guaranteed a hard, face-forward landing. (C. Mason)

A pair of paratrooper knee pads which were worn outside the jump trousers. The parachute technique in practice with the Germans utilized a forward roll in which it was likely that the soldier would hit the ground with his knees at some point during the landing. Pads such as these offered the best protection. (Willi Zahn)

Right: Rear view which shows the manufacturer's RB Nr code and the number "3" which indicates the size. (Willi Zahn)

Left: Unissued pair of late-war knee pads which have been constructed in a coarser material than the knee pads pictured earlier. Right: Rear view of the late-war pads showing details of construction and maker's stamp. Having been stored in this manner, with the straps fastened, for the last 55 years, the straps have become brittle and have lost much of their elastic nature. Note the different colors of leather used to reinforce the fastening post, a common feature on late-war produced items. (Willi Zahn)

This set of knee pads was recently found stored in a factory in Holland and were tied together with a piece of fabric used in their construction. (Willi Zahn)

Above: Though no known wartime photos can confirm the existence of knee pads in splinter pattern, these are made exactly like the olive green pair shown previously. Numerous examples of splinter pattern knee pads can be found which are clearly postwar reproductions, these however are exact in every detail of those known to be original. Below: Markings on the back of the splinter knee pads indicate manufacturer, date and size. (Willi Zahn)

Left: A pair of seldom encountered elbow pads. These pads are also marked with a RB Nr code and a size "3" stamp. Note the rectangular shape of the overall pad which is in no way similar to the tubular shaped tan Italian World War II issue elbow pads often offered on the collector's market as German World War II issue. (Willi Zahn)

This pair of Fallschirmjäger gloves was apparently never issued and retains its paper label with RB Nr code stamp glued inside the cuff. (C. Mason)

Two pair of Fallschirmjäger gloves with later, shorter cuffs. An unlined pair for summer use is on the left and a fur-lined pair for winter use is seen at right. (C. Mason)

Left: Two pair of Fallschirmjäger gloves with earlier, longer cuffs. The pair on the left is fur-lined for winter use, while the pair at right is unlined. (C. Mason)

A pair of unlined brown leather paratrooper gauntlet gloves. Several different styles in regards to length of gauntlet and quality of leather can be encountered. Markings on the inside can include manufacturer, RB Nr code, date and size. (Willi Zahn)

Left: Another pair of unlined gloves. Metal springs were used inside the cuffs to keep the gauntlet tight against the wrist and forearm. As with many paratrooper items, the gloves were specially designed for use in parachuting. Gloves such as these were desired items among U.S. paratroopers, who during the Normandy campaign found them to be a practical item and sometimes wore them. (Willi Zahn)

This page and opposite: Two views of paratroops (left) preparing to load up for the Crete jump at Megara, Greece, and (right) during the Crete invasion. May 1941. (Radovic)

This particular pair of gloves are of the lined style, but the lining does not extend into the gauntlet. The lining appears to be made of rabbit fur, which made them popular for winter wear. (Willi Zahn)

Although not specifically a piece of Fallschirmjäger equipment per se, the six-pocket MP40 magazine pouch is sometimes seen in use by Fallschirmjäger in place of the matched pair of magazine pouches providing three pockets on either side. Another version exists with individual pocket flaps for each of the six pockets. Both are considered rare. (C. Mason)

Rear side of the MP40 six-pocket magazine pouch. These are believed to have been designed for assault troops and assault engineers. It's possible that wear on the front of the body was intended to prevent interference with grenade bags. (C. Mason)

This close up of the side of the MP40 six-pocket magazine pouch shows the formed leather insert on the edge of the flap to protect the magazines from dirt and weather. (C. Mason)

Textbook example of the early war cloth carrying bag for the gas mask. Of interest are the Waffenamt ink stamp on the snap closure flap and the unique bone-shaped insert in the zipper pull.This enabled the wearer to distinguish his gas mask from any other zipper in complete darkness. (C. Mason)

The cloth gas mask carrying bag turned inside out, with some of the gas mask accessories it was issued with. Seen here are spare lenses and the gas mask lens cleaning cloth. Of particular interest is the molded green rubber plug sewn into the seam of the bag. Any gas mask bag without this plug is a post-war reproduction. (C. Mason)

Late-war gas mask bag which was specially designed for Fallschirmjäger use. Gas mask bags were used in lieu of the standard Wehrmacht issue gas mask can, which could have caused injury to paratroopers upon landing. Though slight variations of this bag were used during the war, this style bag was often seen in use on the Normandy front. (Willi Zahn)

An unzipped view of the gas mask bag illustrating how the gas mask was stored. The snaps in this particular bag are marked "Prym", and the flap of the bag is marked with the manufacturers code and a waffenamt marking. The code represents the company of "Fatra AG" in Napajedl/Mähren, a manufacturer of specialist rubberwear and containers. (Willi Zahn)

Above: Numerous styles and variations of Kar 98k ammo bandoleers were in use throughout the war. The first on the left is an early war version in blue/gray. The next is a pre-war version in blue/gray with square flaps. The third is a late-war 1944 dated version in olive tan cotton, and the last is a standard mid-war style in Luftwaffe splinter pattern. Close examination of photographs taken during the Crete campaign shows an extremely high number of square flap bandoleers still in use. (Willi Zahn)

Right: Bandoleer worn by paratroopers on Crete, May 1941.

Opposite: Paratrooper with MP40 and MP38/40 magazine pouch.

An example of the very late K98 rifle ammunition bandoleers produced at the end of the war from bits of scrap fabric, a classic indication of the declining standards and stopgap measures forced on German industry by war's end. (C. Mason)

A set of hand grenade bags with white plastic "RiRi" zippers of the style common on many jump smocks. This set has a RB Nr code stamped on the inside of one of the openings. (Willi Zahn)

Standard issue map case with typical contents. Of special interest is the March 1941 dated military-issue map of Crete marked "Sonderausgabe" ("special issue"). (C. Mason)

Opposite below: Three different color/fabric variations of Luftwaffe splinter pattern grenade bags. These bags usually come in sets of two, but for some reason these bags have been cut from their respective matching second halves and have also had their attaching straps cut off. The attaching straps on all three are made from a black cotton webbing, based on what little remains of the webbing at the side seams of the bags. Like splinter jump smocks, ground division jackets, bandoleers and helmet covers, the Luftwaffe splinter pattern varies little from the Heer pattern, in that the pattern is a little tighter on the Luftwaffe version. (Willi Zahn)

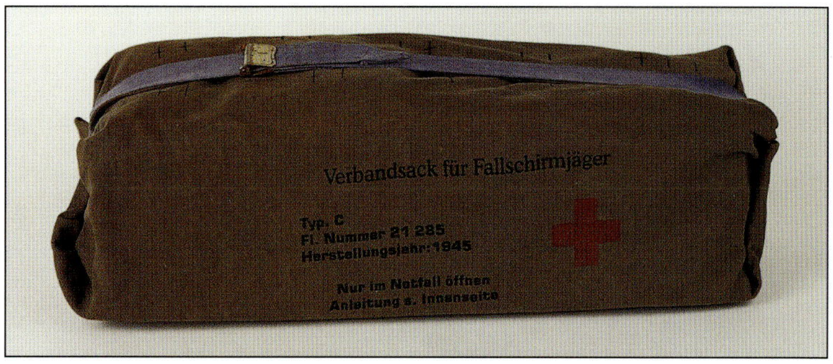

The Verbandsack designed for Fallschirmjäger use as a substitute for the heavy metal or wood Verbandkasten of ground troops. It is marked "Typ. C" and dated 1945. (C. Mason)

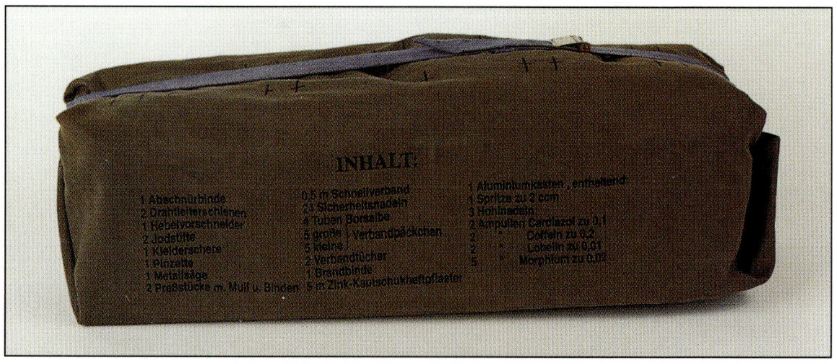

The list of contents of the Fallschirmjäger medical kit is printed on the opposite side from the nomenclature panel. Instructions for use are printed on the inside. (C. Mason)

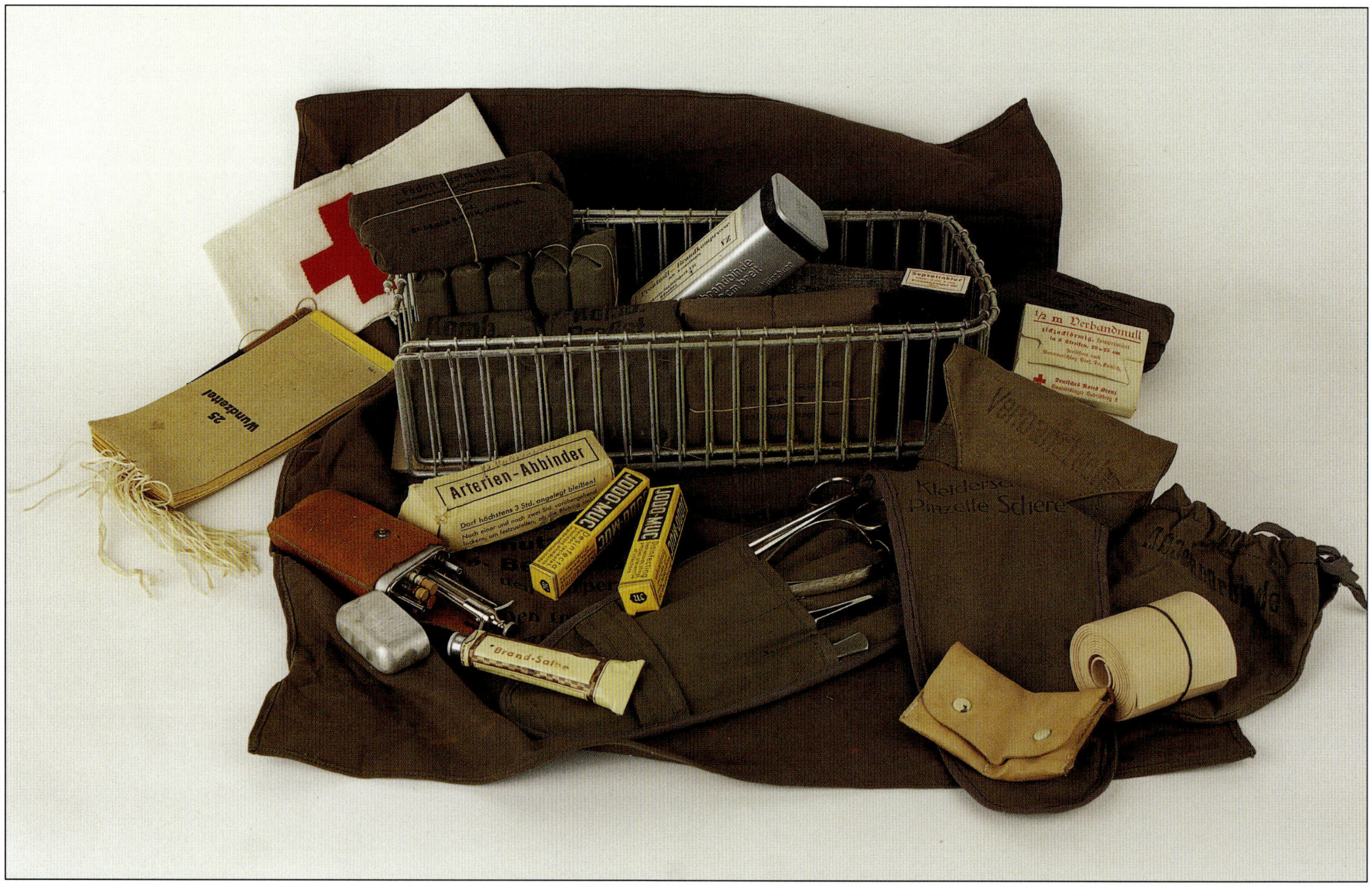

The Verbandsack could be carried into action by one man and provided the bare necessities for treating combat wounds in the absence of an organized forward aid station, including limited surgical tools and a hypodermic kit with syringe and vials of morphine which the instructions indicate are for "doctor's use only." (C. Mason)

Above: An example of the canvas protective cover for the K98 rifle with six leather tab and stud closures. Bands of pressed and formed horsehair at either end were reasonably effective in sealing out dirt and rain. The cover is not generally thought to be a jump cover per se, but it was issued to some extent to paratroops, and may have been used to protect the rifle when carried on jumps after the Crete campaign. (C. Mason)

Right: Field-made protective cover for the MP40 machine pistol, made from shelter quarter material. Such expedients were commonly produced at the unit level. One or two tailors and cobblers were assigned to every battalion to repair equipment and clothing. (C. Mason)

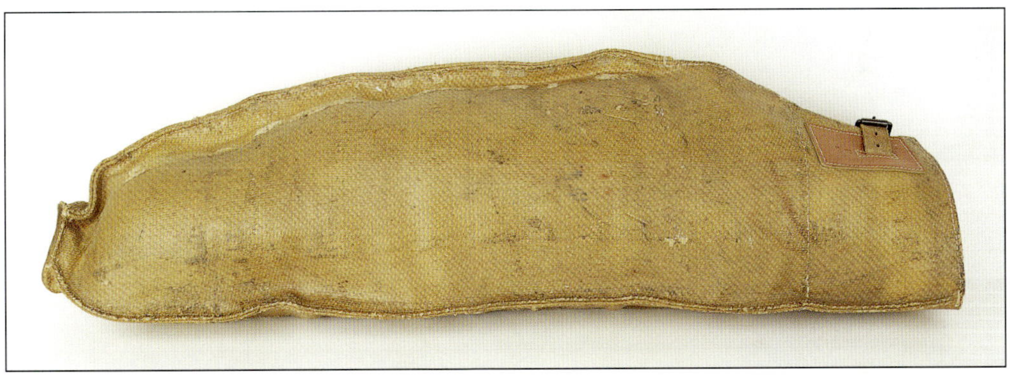

Right: Rare protective parachute jump cover for the MP40 machine pistol. It is made of waterproofed canvas with a leather buckle closure. (C. Mason)

Detail of the closure device shows the Waffenamt acceptance stamp in the leather reinforcement. A mucilage-based coating, applied as waterproofing, has yellowed and deteriorated with age. The horsehair padding in paratrooper helmet liners, mucilage glues and such waterproof coatings were typical industrial uses for horse carcasses during the Third Reich era. (C. Mason)

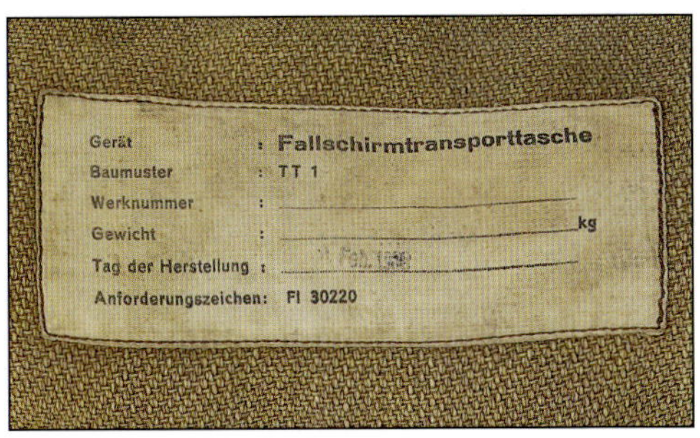

The cloth nomenclature label on the carrying bag for the RZ1 personnel parachute. Carrying bags for later models omitted these labels. The bags were carried only on training jumps to assist the jumper in carrying the parachute off the drop zone for inspection and repacking. (C. Mason)

Close up of the top flap of an RZ16 parachute carrying bag showing a hand painted tactical marking for parachute engineers (Fallschirmpioniere). (C. Mason)

A typical Fallschirmjäger Erkennungsmarke, or in GI parlance, "dogtag," which identified the individual. Soldiers often purchased leather pouches like this one to make wearing the disc against the skin more comfortable in cold weather. (C. Mason)

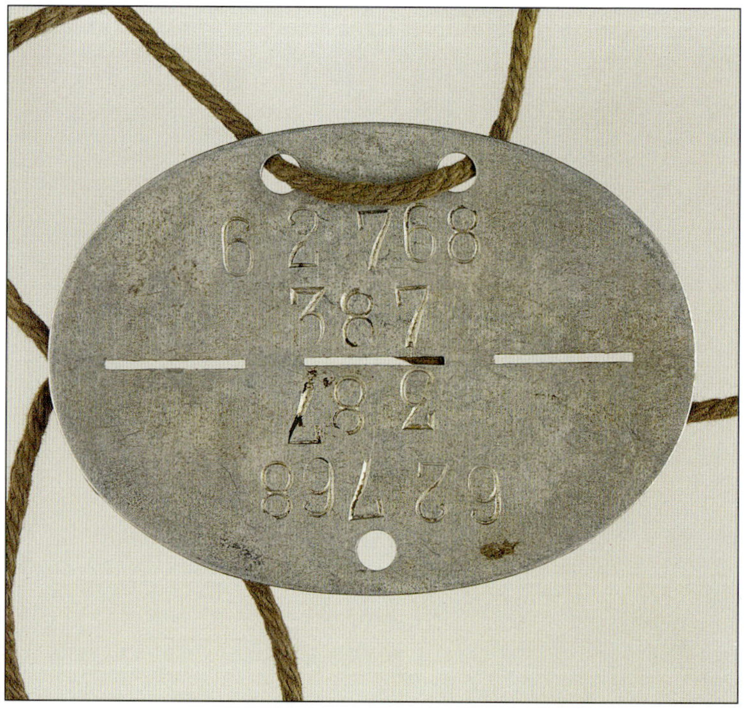

Luftwaffe dogtags for flight personnel and paratroops were encoded with a series of five or six digit numbers, known as MOB Nummern, which identified units down to the company level. The unit number is stamped above, and the individual's Stammrollen Nummer, or personal number, is the three-digit number below that. This was done for security purposes for all personnel who could fly behind enemy lines in the course of duty. All Fallschirmjäger dogtags conform to this numbering system, and any dogtag with letters instead of numbers is a post-war reproduction. Because this tag has no blood group indicated, it may be unissued. (C. Mason)

Another example of the Fallschirmjäger Erkennungsmarke. This has a relatively low Stammrollen number, indicating the individual was one of the original members of the company. Also visible are his blood type ("A") and his gas mask size. (C. Mason)

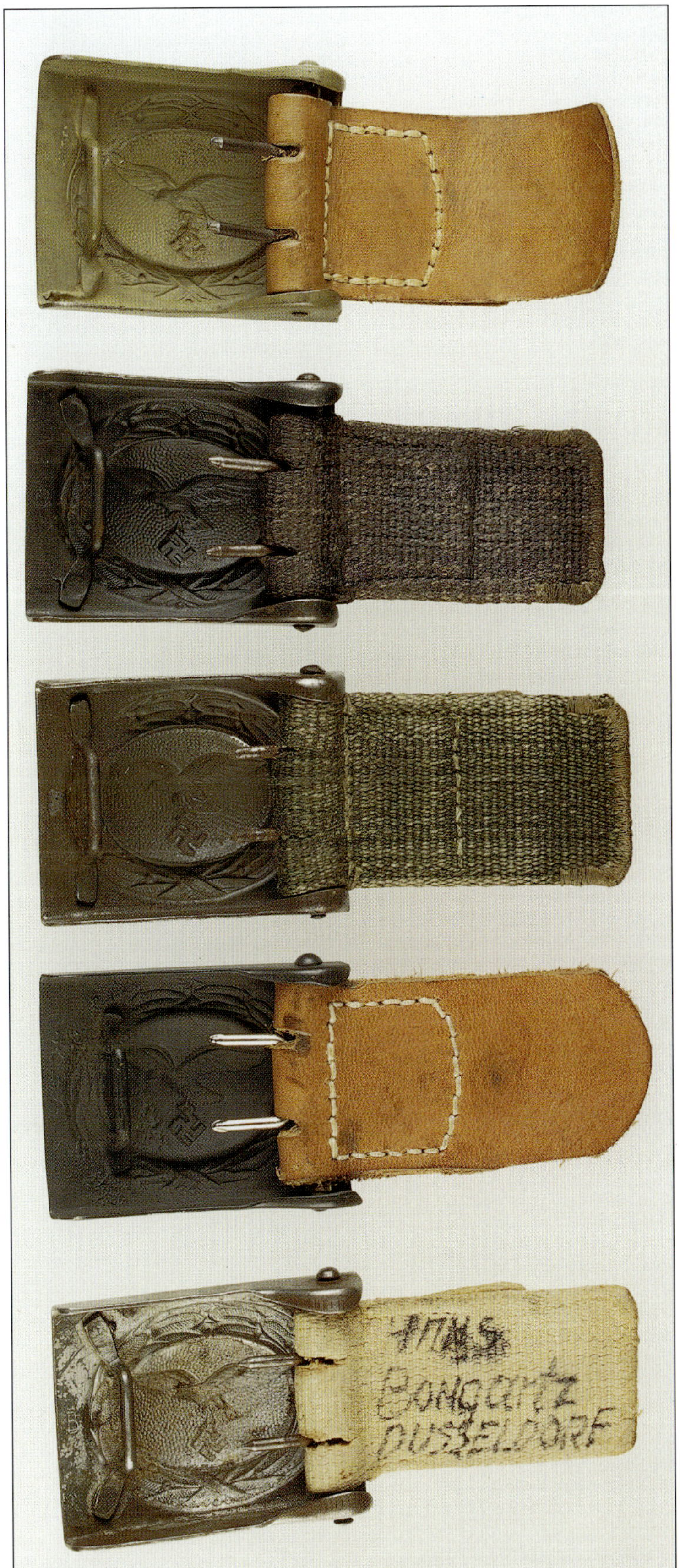

A few examples of some of the variations of the Luftwaffe buckle worn by paratroopers. These five examples are all dated either 1941 or 1942. Buckles worn before those years are normally of the unpainted aluminum style. Until recently reproduction buckles were not very convincing, however in the past several years excellent copies of the tropical olive tan buckles have appeared on the market. (Willi Zahn)

Three examples of the gravity knife issued to all Luftwaffe flight personnel. It would be used to cut away shroud lines in the event of entanglement after a parachute landing and could be operated one-handed, a precaution still observed by many parachute forces today. The knife at left is the second model of the gravity knife. Fittings were blued to prevent glare from the metal, and the pushbutton allowed the knife to be disassembled for repair. Of interest is the RB Nr code on the blade. Two of the most common makers of the early knives are also shown, Weyersberg and SMF, as are three types of lanyards issued with the knives. (C. Mason)

Three views of the RZ20 parachute being readied prior to a training jump.

Above: A complete RZ20 parachute as used by the Fallschirmtruppen from mid- to late-war. The stamping of "Ju 52" and "He 111" indicates the type of aircraft this chute was designed to be deployed from. The nylon rope with large hook is the static line, and was hooked on to a support wire inside the aircraft. The ropes present on the sides are the canopy risers. (Willi Zahn)

Right: A view of the tag sewn to the bottom of the RZ20 parachute. The tag indicates that it is a jump chute for use by the paratroopers, and has a camouflage canopy. (Willi Zahn)

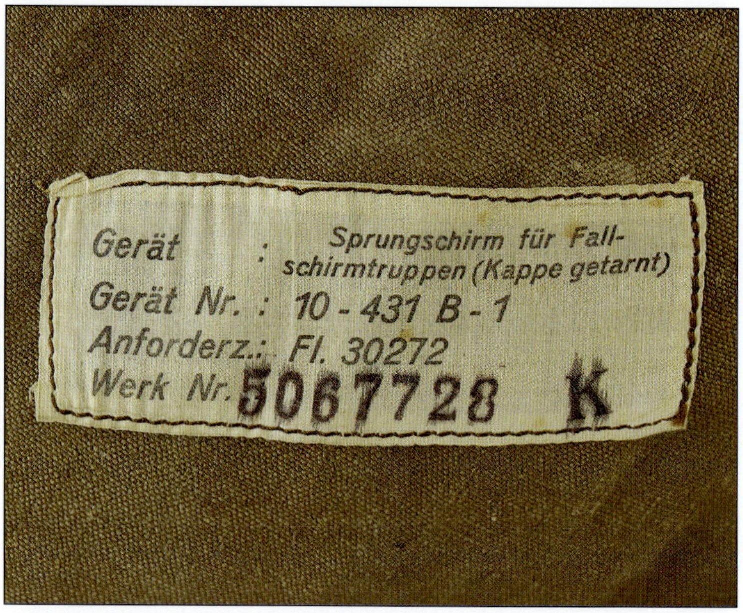

Harness of the RZ20. Note how the rope canopy risers are hooked to the middle of each side of the harness. This demonstrates why the German paratroopers utilized a unique style when exiting the aircraft. As the risers are in the middle of the back, the paratrooper must leap horizontally from the aircraft in the face down position, thereby allowing the chute to deploy properly. Surviving films of Fallschirmtruppen deploying from aircraft clearly demonstrate this technique unique to German paratroopers. (Willi Zahn)

Parachute carrying bag. The chute was carried in this bag, which was then placed inside the storage container. (Willi Zahn)

Late-war ordnance tan airtight storage container for the RZ20 parachute. Parachutes used by the Fallschirmtruppen were stored in these at various airfields. Many of these containers were used by U.S. veterans after the Normandy campaign to send their acquired souvenirs home. Parachutes were stored at various Luftwaffe airfields in France, where several Fallschirmjäger Divisions received parachute training in 1943 and early 1944. (Willi Zahn)

Lid of the storage can. The top line indicates that the can is a weather proof container for personnel parachutes. The last line indicates the container was made in 1944 with the code of "ebr" identifying the manufacturer. Note that the type of chute "RZ20" is stamped on the lid. (Willi Zahn)

Drop cannisters being prepared for Crete invasion (above), and during Crete invasion (below). Note shock absorber rings at left rear in photo above, and also the medical supply identification markings on the foreground cannister. The photo below shows a communications set up. Note cannister wheels and tow bar.

Chapter Five

Documents, Books, Misc.

Far left: The Fallschirmjäger were a part of popular culture in wartime Germany. This adventure story for boys features a Fallschirmjäger theme. (C. Mason)

Left: Two-hundred copies of this photo album were printed for the men of the 3. Kompanie, Fallschirm- Flak-MG Bataillon in December, 1941 as keepsakes. This copy is numbered 129. (C. Mason)

Right: This hand-made keepsake was presented to Lieutenant Colonel Gustav Wilke by his men on the occasion of his birthday. (C. Mason)

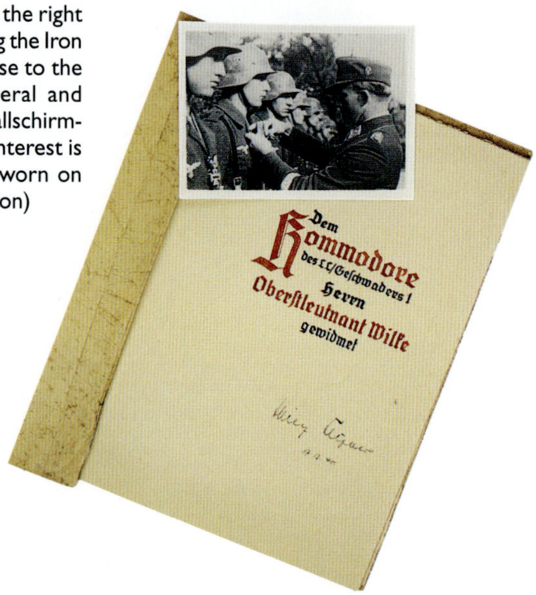

Right: Wilke, seen on the right of the photo awarding the Iron Cross to his men, rose to the rank of Major General and commanded the 2. Fallschirm-Division. Of special interest is the "Meindl Badge" worn on his M43 cap. (C. Mason)

Left: This popular cartoon and verse book, entitled "So Wird Mann Fallschirmjäger" ("This is How One Becomes a Paratrooper") was filled with humorous sketches of training, parachuting and barracks life. (C. Mason)

Above: Many books about the Fallschirmjäger were published during the Third Reich. This one, "Kreta, Sieg der Kühnsten" (Crete: Victory of the Boldest), is best known for the splinter pattern camouflage cover. The dust jacket is rare. (C. Mason)

Above: This was the classified packing manual for the weapons and equipment canisters published in April, 1942. This copy was issued to a headquarters signals unit. (C. Mason)

Far right: This is one of the rarest of the Fallschirmjäger books produced by Nazi Germany, as it was printed very late in the war. (C. Mason)

Right: One of the more common books on the Fallschirmjäger, this one was written by Gericke as an overview of the paratroops and their history. (C. Mason)

Left: One of the early adventure books for children, this small format hardcover depicts the army parachutist badge on the cover. (C. Mason)

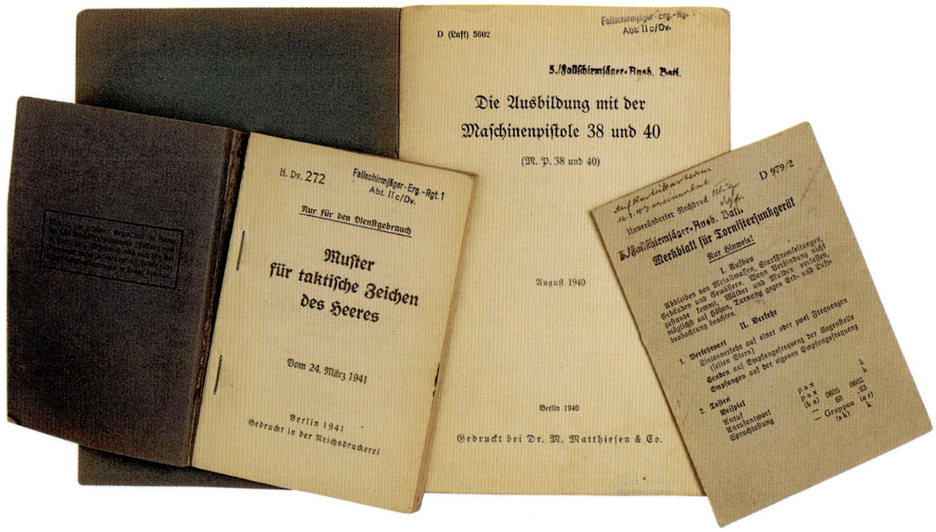

Left: An unusual and rare relic of Fallschirmjäger propaganda, this is the Dutch edition of Schmidt's "Fallschirmjäger von Dombas," released under the title "Parachutisten Grijpen In" in Rotterdam in 1942. (C. Mason)

Above: Examples of three technical manuals issued to Fallschirmjäger training and replacement units. (C. Mason)

Two above and two at right: Members of the Fallschirmtruppen were often featured on the covers of various wartime German new magazines. These publications offer a unique insight into what the German public was told regarding the exploits of the paratroopers, and how the war was going. (Willi Zahn)

Far right: Original example of a short history of the Fallschirmtruppen, which was printed in 1943. This book has many photographs and was recently reprinted and translated by Schiffer Publishing. (Willi Zahn)

Right: Wartime recruiting pamphlet stating that the, "Paratroopers are calling you." (Willi Zahn)

Above: Many short books were published during the war years detailing the exploits of the Fallschirmtruppen during the early campaigns. Many of these were directed at members of the various youth organizations present during the Third Reich. (Willi Zahn)

Right: A wartime published account by a famous paratrooper, Walter Gericke, who distinguished himself throughout the entire war. (Willi Zahn)

The route to becoming a Fallschirmjäger often began with a recruiting booklet like this one. The title, "Willst Du Fallschirmjäger Werden?" translates to "Do You Want to Become a Paratrooper?" Inside the booklet was a fill-in-the-blanks volunteer form which a soldier wishing to become a paratrooper could fill out and mail to the XI. Fliegerkorps. (C. Mason)

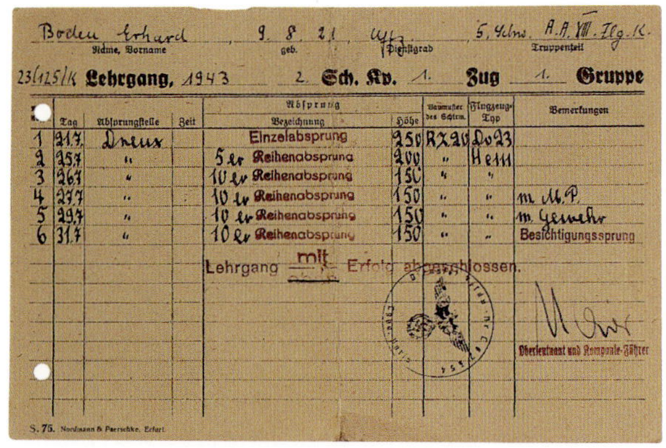
Boden Erhard 9. 8. 21 Uffz. 5./Ulns. A.A. VIII. Flg. K.

23/125/K Lehrgang, 1943 2. Sch. Kp. 1. Zug 1. Gruppe

Tag	Absprungstelle	Zeit	Bezeichnung	Höhe	Baumuster des Schirm.	Flugzeug-Typ	Bemerkungen
1 21.7.	Dreux		Einzelabsprung	250	RZ20	Do 23	
2 25.7.	"		5er Reihenabsprung	200	"	He 111	
3 26.7.	"		10er Reihenabsprung	150	"	"	
4 27.7.	"		10er Reihenabsprung	150	"	"	m. M.P.
5 29.7.	"		10er Reihenabsprung	150	"	"	m. Gewehr
6 31.7.	"		10er Reihenabsprung	150	"	-	Besichtigungssprung

Lehrgang mit Erfolg abgeschlossen.

Oberleutnant und Kompanie-Führer

Once accepted and selected for parachute training, the volunteer was ordered to jump school, where his jumps were recorded on a record card like this one. This card shows the student made a highly-unusual jump from a Dornier Do 23, a very unorthodox aircraft for parachute training. (C. Mason)

Left: The first Fallschirmjäger had their flights and parachute jumps recorded in a Flugbuch (Flight Log) in the same manner as pilots until the introduction of the jump card. (C. Mason)

Below: The interior of the Flugbuch, this one issued to Jäger Kurt Scheibe, records all the details of his six qualifying jumps during a seventeen day period in August, 1940. Any military parachute descent counted toward the six required. Late in the war, pilots transferring to the paratroops who had made emergency jumps received credit for those jumps at jump school. (C. Mason)

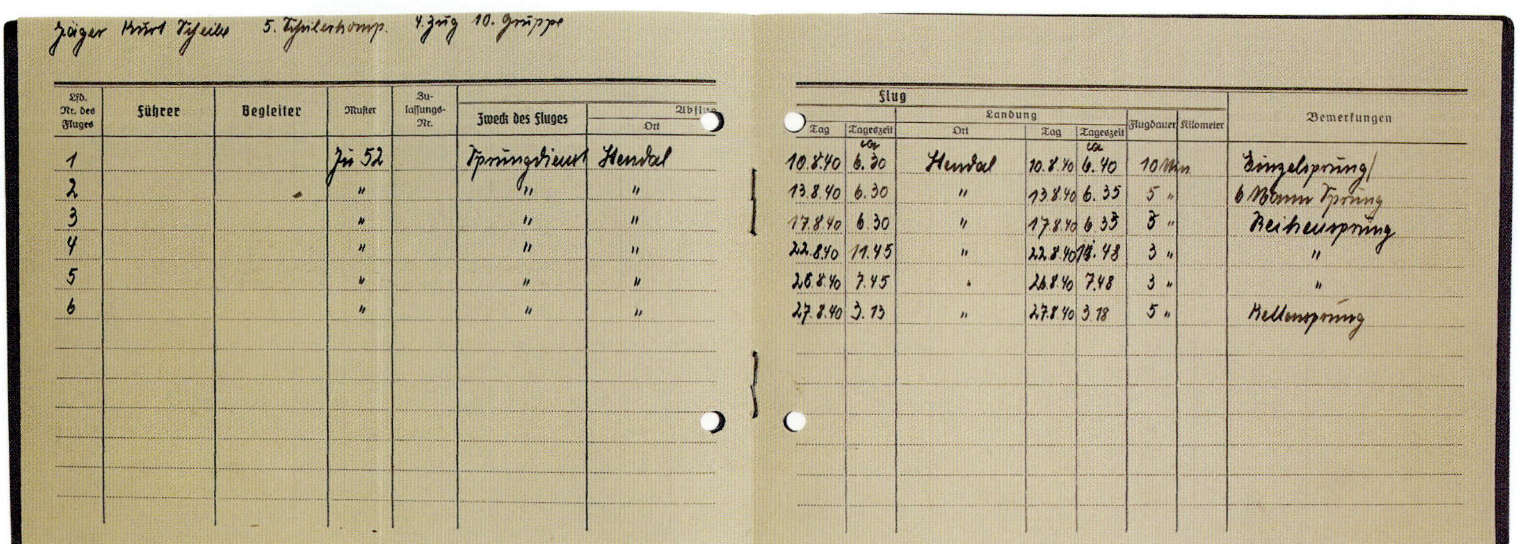
Jäger Kurt Scheibe 5. Schülerkomp. 4. Zug 10. Gruppe

Lfd. Nr. des Fluges	Führer	Begleiter	Muster	Zulassungs-Nr.	Zweck des Fluges	Abflug Ort	Abflug Tag	Abflug Tageszeit	Landung Ort	Landung Tag	Landung Tageszeit	Flugdauer	Kilometer	Bemerkungen
1			Ju 52		Sprungdienst	Stendal	10.8.40	6.30	Stendal	10.8.40	6.40	10 Min		Einzelsprung
2			"		"	"	13.8.40	6.30	"	13.8.40	6.35	5 "		6 Mann Sprung
3			"		"	"	17.8.40	6.30	"	17.8.40	6.33	3 "		Reihensprung
4			"		"	"	22.8.40	11.45	"	22.8.40	11.48	3 "		"
5			"		"	"	26.8.40	7.45	"	26.8.40	7.48	3 "		"
6			"		"	"	27.8.40	3.13	"	27.8.40	3.18	5 "		Kettensprung

Right: A typical example of pages four and five of a Fallschirmjäger Soldbuch showing the units the man served in. This paratrooper went to all the various training and jump school commands before joining Fallschirmjäger Regiment 2 and serving in the 5. and 8. Kompanien. (C. Mason)

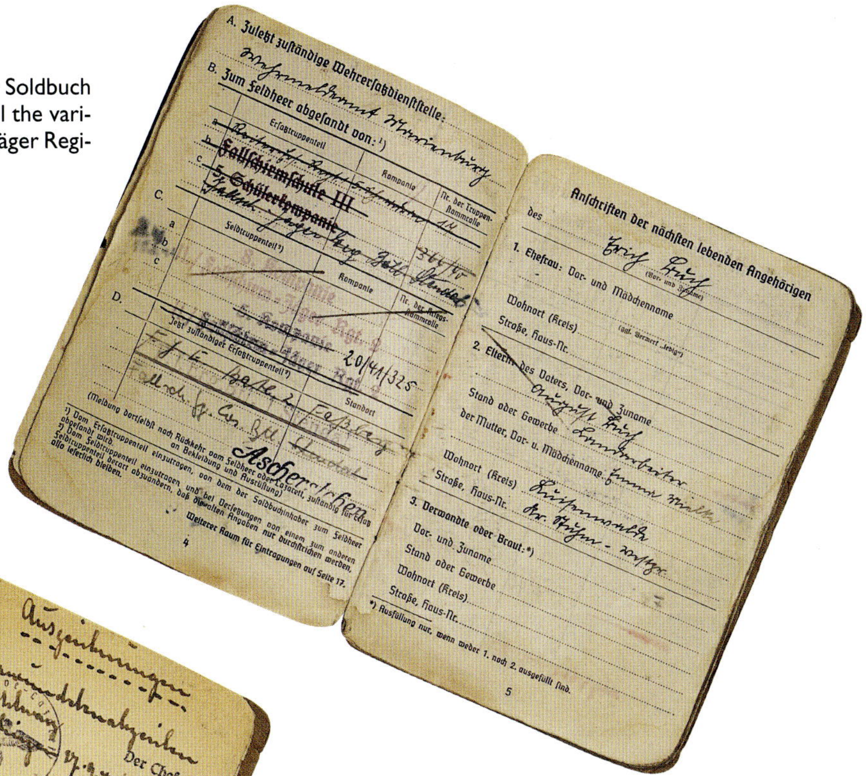

Above: Page twenty-two of the Soldbuch became the standard awards page for the Luftwaffe Soldbuch, as the designers of the document omitted this feature. This example shows how the awards often spilled over onto other pages, such as this extra page glued in as a continuation page for further decorations. On these two pages are entered the paratrooper badge, EKII, Russian Front Medal, the EKI and the Wound Badge in Black. (C. Mason)

Right: Additional awards received by this Fallschirmjäger were entered on page twenty-one after page twenty-two filled up, a common practice. Here, the Ground Combat Badge of the Luftwaffe and the Kreta Cufftitle were entered before the extra page seen in the previous photograph was glued in to save room for pay entries. (C. Mason)

The Soldbuch (paybook) and Fallschirmschützenschein (parachuting license) to a Oberleutnant and company commander of the 2nd Fallschirmjäger Division. Soldbuchs contain a wealth of information to the historian, and those of paratroopers even list all the specialized equipment issued to them. (Willi Zahn)

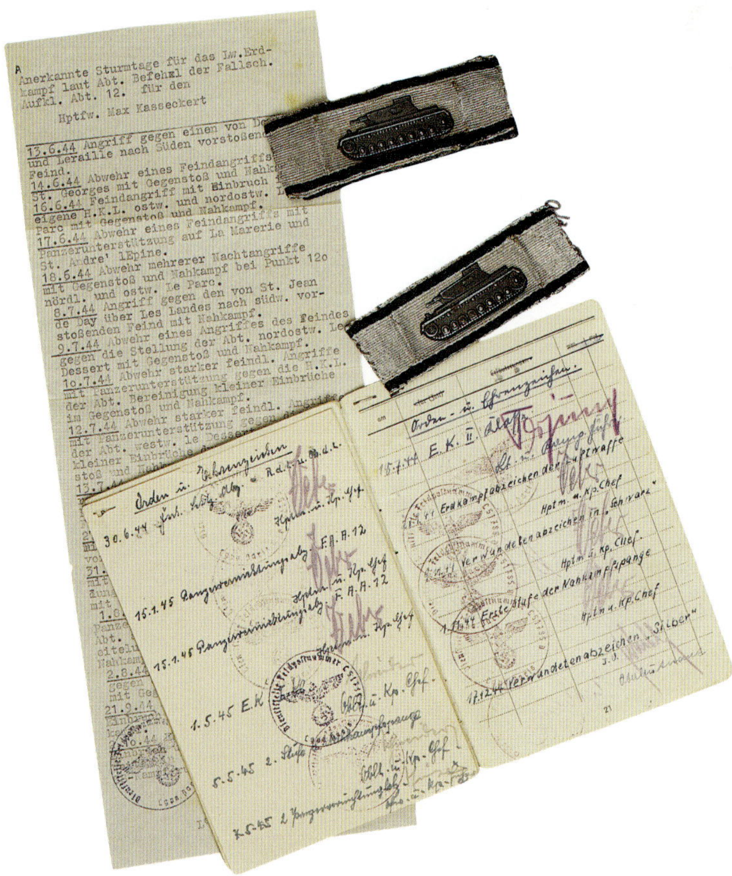

The Soldbuch of a Fallschirmjäger tank buster, Leutnant Max Kasseckert. On the left hand page are entered four of the six tank destruction strips he earned during the war for knocking out tanks while acting alone with infantry weapons. Like most tank busters, Kasseckert wore all silver Panzervernichtungsabzeichenen, and had never heard of the gold version of the award until he was located and interviewed in 1995. Also seen is his listing of close combat days. (C. Mason)

Left: Leutnant Max Kasseckert came up through the ranks of the Fallschirmjäger and earned a battlefield commission, an increasingly common solution to the terrible casualty rates among junior officers. The entry in his Soldbuch (on a page which has come loose since the war) shows the award of the German Cross in Gold on 17 May, 1945 signed by Major Jungwirth, commander of Fallschirm Aufklärungs Abteilung 12 at the time. (C. Mason)

Below: The Wehrpass of Knights Cross bearer Albert Stecken. Unlike the Soldbuch, which was normally carried on the soldier, the Wehrpass was maintained by higher headquarters, and was used to regenerate the Soldbuch in the event of loss or damage. (C. Mason)

Left: The Soldbuch of Feldwebel Adolf Reininghaus, who was awarded the Knights Cross during the siege of Brest in 1944 by General Bernhard Ramcke. (C. Mason)

Above: The award of the Knights Cross came near the end of the siege of Brest, and was never entered in Reininghaus's Soldbuch before he was captured by American forces. He spent the remainder of the war in POW camps in the U.S., where his studio portrait wearing the award was probably taken. (C. Mason)

Left: The Soldbuch and Ausweis of Feldwebel Gustav Petschek. This book was issued as a replacement for a damaged, lost or filled original. Petschek's paratrooper badge is visible in his Ausweis photo. (C. Mason)

Four typical examples of the Fallschirmschützenschein. Germany remains a heavily regulated society today, as it was during the war years. Licenses were, and are, required for many things, including parachuting. This oilcloth document was essentially the equivalent of a drivers license for parachute jumping. In theory it was renewed each year, but this seems to have been rarely observed. (C. Mason)

Above: The Soldbuch, drivers license and Fallschirmschützenschein of Unteroffizier Johann Ingensiep, a veteran of the Brigade Ramcke in North Africa and the Ardennes jump with von der Heydte in the Battle of the Bulge. Ingensiep died from disease in a U.S. POW camp in Germany several weeks after the war. (C. Mason)

Below: Another typical Fallschirmjäger Soldbuch and Erkennungsmarke. This example has an extra page appended to the bottom of page twenty-two, with an entry for the Kreta cufftitle, in addition to entries for the Russian Front medal, the Wound Badge in Black and the Ground Combat Badge of the Luftwaffe. (C. Mason)

Left: The Soldbuch was a pay book, military record and ID card all rolled into one. Most Soldbücher contained identity photographs of the bearer on the inside front cover, although examples are sometimes seen without them. Unlike the Wehrpass, which regulations stipulated contain a photograph in civilian clothing, the Soldbuch was to contain a photograph in uniform without any headgear. Originally created without photographs, the wartime requirement to contain them was a security measure. The first page contained the individual's name, rank, dogtag number, blood group, gas mask size, and military service number (Wehrnummer). (C. Mason)

This group of artifacts belonged to Fallschirmjäger Stabsarzt Dr. Karl Semm (his boots appear on page 140). Semm served as a frontline aid station surgeon with a paratroop reconnaissance section on the western front (Fallschirm Aufklärungs Abteilung 12). He earned the Iron Cross 1st and 2nd Class for heroism under fire and saved the lives of countless young men on both sides of the conflict in 1944 and 1945. He survived several wounds and practiced medicine for another fifty years after the war. (C. Mason)

The Soldbuch of Unteroffizier KOB Herbert Reinersmann, who earned nineteen medals and decorations, including the German Cross in Gold, and served in every major campaign of the Fallschirmjäger and on every front. In the photograph he is seen wearing both the Kreta and the Afrika cufftitle. Reinersmann was killed in action several days before the end of the war. (C. Mason)

The Soldbuch and photographs of Major Horst Zimmermann, the last commanding officer of Fallschirmjäger Regiment 5 in Tunisia. In the wartime photograph at bottom center (printed backwards from the negative), Zimmermann has just received the German Cross in Gold on the Russian Front. Zimmermann was ordered to surrender his unit in North Africa and spent the remainder of the war in American POW camps. (C. Mason)

Verleihungsurkunde

Ich verleihe dem

Gefreiten

Werner Meyer

das Abzeichen für

Fallschirmschützen

Berlin, den 24. August 1942

Der Reichsminister der Luftfahrt und Oberbefehlshaber der Luftwaffe

I. A.:

Der Chef des Luftwaffenpersonalamts

General der Flieger

Nr. VIII 42

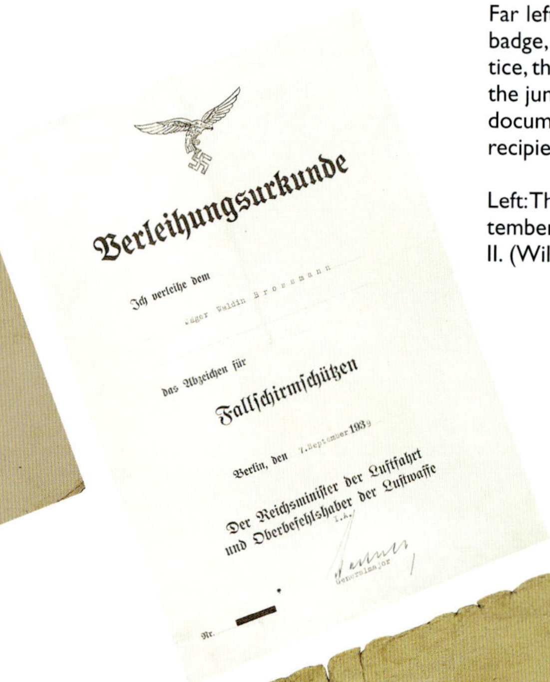

Verleihungsurkunde

Ich verleihe dem

Jäger Waldin Brossmann

das Abzeichen für

Fallschirmschützen

Berlin, den 7. September 1939

Der Reichsminister der Luftfahrt und Oberbefehlshaber der Luftwaffe

Far left: A typical early award document for the parachutist badge, or Fallschirmschützenabzeichen. Unlike the U.S. practice, these documents were processed after the student left the jump school for his unit. It often took months for these documents and the accompanying badge to catch up to the recipient in the field. (C. Mason)

Left: The award of the paratrooper badge was made on September 7, 1939, just days after the official start of World War II. (Willi Zahn)

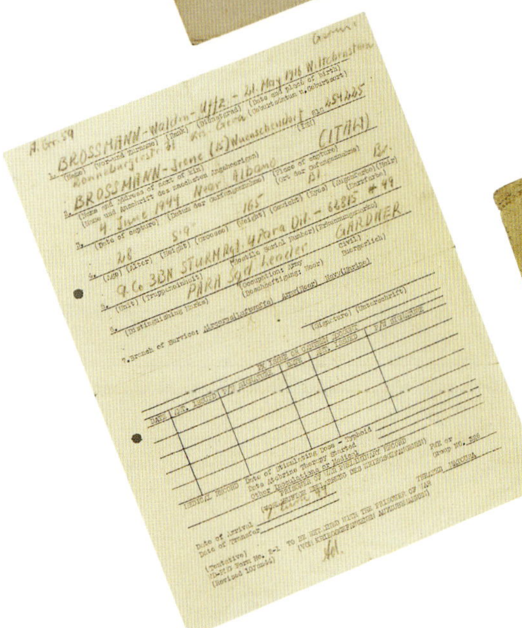

Above: This captured paper is to the same paratrooper named in the earlier documents, which shows that he was captured on June 4, 1944 in Albano, Italy, as a squad leader in the 9th company, 3rd battalion, Sturm Regiment in the 4th Paratrooper Division. Though the Sturm Regiment at this point of the war was officially known as the 12th Fallschirmjäger Regiment, early members such as this paratrooper who had fought with them during and after Crete, continued to call the regiment by its traditional name. (Willi Zahn)

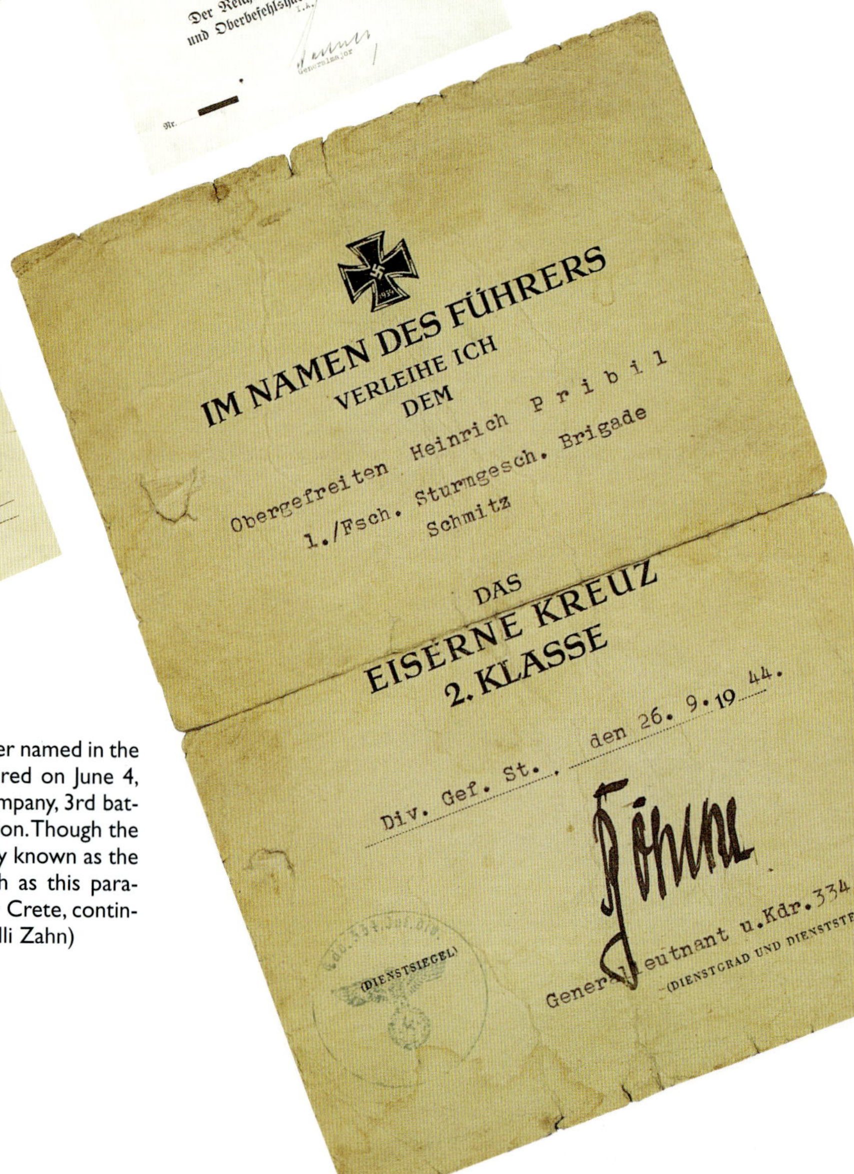

IM NAMEN DES FÜHRERS

VERLEIHE ICH

DEM

Obergefreiten Heinrich Pribil

1./Fsch. Sturmgesch. Brigade

Schmitz

DAS

EISERNE KREUZ

2. KLASSE

Div. Gef. St., den 26. 9. 1944.

Generalleutnant u. Kdr. 334. Inf. Div.

(DIENSTGRAD UND DIENSTSTELLUNG)

(DIENSTSIEGEL)

Above: A rare award document to a man in Fallschirmsturmgeschütz Brigade Schmitz, an assault gun unit formed in Italy as part of the I. Fallschirm Korps using confiscated Italian Semovente M42L da 105/25 assault guns, signed by the Commanding General of Infantry Division 334. (C. Mason)

Right: An example of a promotion document presented to a Fallschirmjäger. It certifies that Feldwebel Heinrich Gabbey of Fallschirmjäger Regiment 6 has been promoted to Oberfeldwebel. It is signed by the Regimental Commander, Major von der Heydte, who would later lead the ill-fated final parachute operation in the Ardennes offensive in December 1944. (C. Mason)

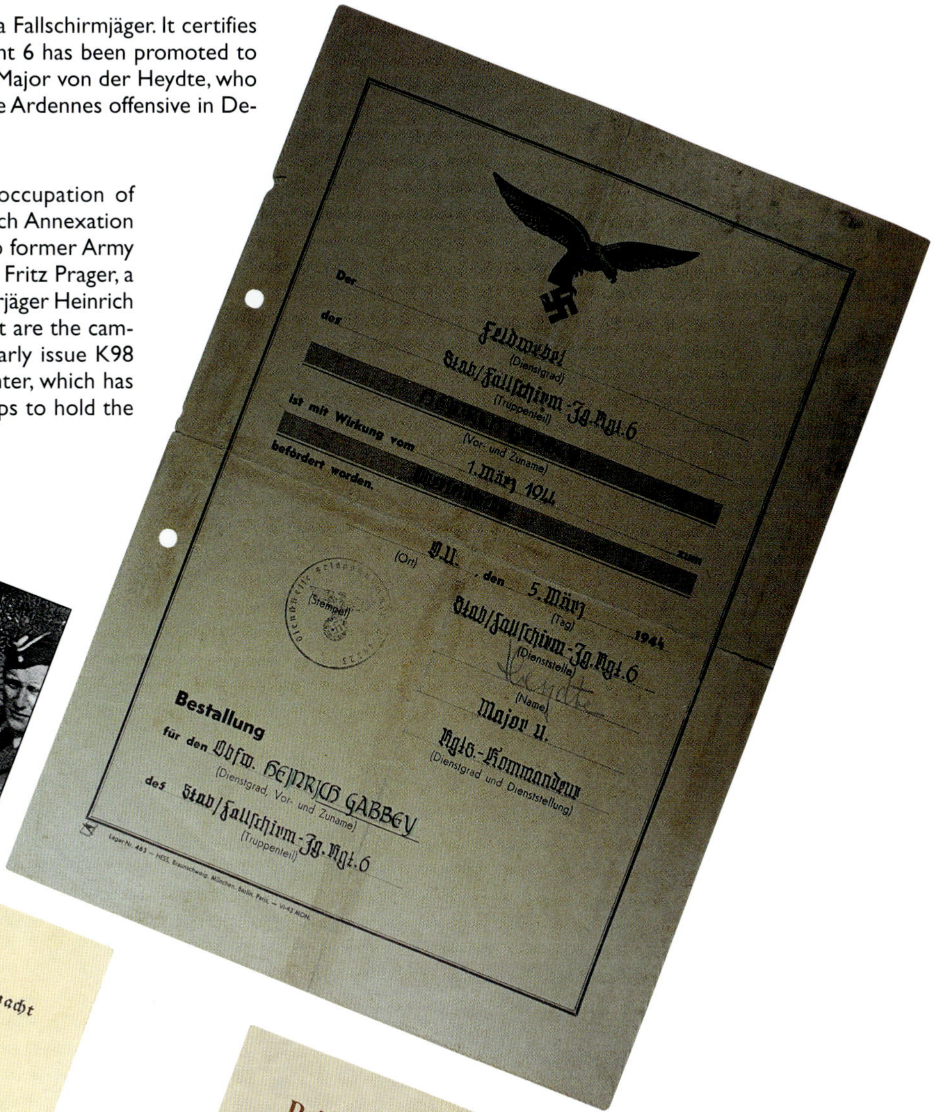
Der
Feldwebel
(Dienstgrad)
des Stab/Fallschirm-Jg.Rgt.6
(Truppenteil)
(Vor- und Zuname)
ist mit Wirkung vom 1.März 1944
befördert worden.
O.U. (Ort), den 5.März (Tag) 1944
Stab/Fallschirm-Jg.Rgt.6
(Dienststelle)
(Name)
Major u.
Rgts.-Kommandeur
(Dienstgrad und Dienststellung)
(Stempel)
Bestallung
für den Obfw. HEINRICH GABBEY
(Dienstgrad, Vor- und Zuname)
des Stab/Fallschirm-Jg.Rgt.6
(Truppenteil)

Bottom: Fallschirmjäger Regiment 1 participated in the occupation of Czechoslovakia in 1938. This award document for the Czech Annexation Medal (Medaille zur Erinnerung an den 1. Oktober 1938) to former Army Fallschirmjäger Heinrich Gabbey was signed by Hauptmann Fritz Prager, a Knights Cross bearer who died of cancer in 1940. Below: Oberjäger Heinrich Gabbey stands on the far left in this photograph. Of interest are the camouflage paint schemes on the two helmets, and the very early issue K98 ammunition bandoleer worn by the paratrooper in the center, which has only narrow cloth strips with snaps instead of complete flaps to hold the ammunition in place. (C. Mason)

Im Namen
des Führers und Obersten Befehlshabers der Wehrmacht
verleihe ich
dem
Gefreiten Heinrich Gabbey
die Medaille zur Erinnerung an den 1. Oktober 1938
mit Spange*
Berlin, den 20. Juni 1939.
Für die Richtigkeit:
(Name, Dienstgrad und Dienststellung)
* Bei Nichtverleihung streichen.
Nr. 1345 /39 A
(Siegel)
Der Kommandeur der Flieger-Division 7
Student
Generalmajor

BESITZZEUGNIS
DEM
Oberjäger Hans Wartelsteiner
2./ Fallschirm - Jäger Rgt. 15
VERLEIHE ICH DAS
ERDKAMPFABZEICHEN
DER LUFTWAFFE
Gef.Stand, 2.10.1944
Oberstleutnant u.Div.-Führer

Right: One of the most elaborate and graphically interesting versions of the many styles of award document for the Erdkampfabzeichen, or Ground Combat Badge, of the Luftwaffe. This example was signed by Oberst Kurt Gröschke, who received the Knights Cross in June of 1944. (C. Mason)

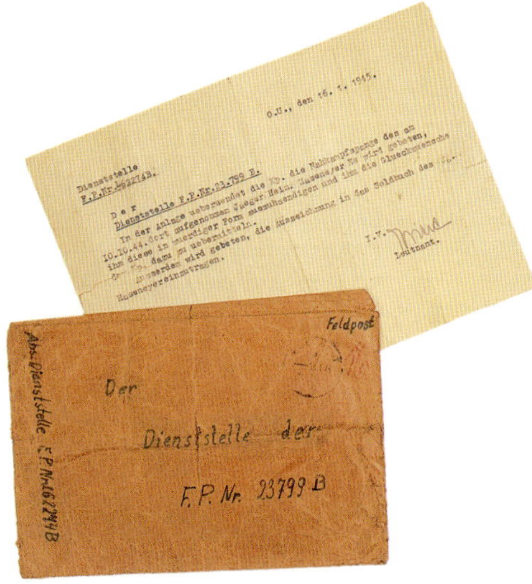

Above: This document was sent by the company commander of the 15. Kompanie, Fallschirmjäger Regiment 11, together with a Nahkampfspange (Close Combat Clasp) in Bronze, in the manila envelope to a field hospital with the request that the award be presented to a Fallschirmjäger rifleman recovering there, and also requests that the award be entered in his Soldbuch. (C. Mason)

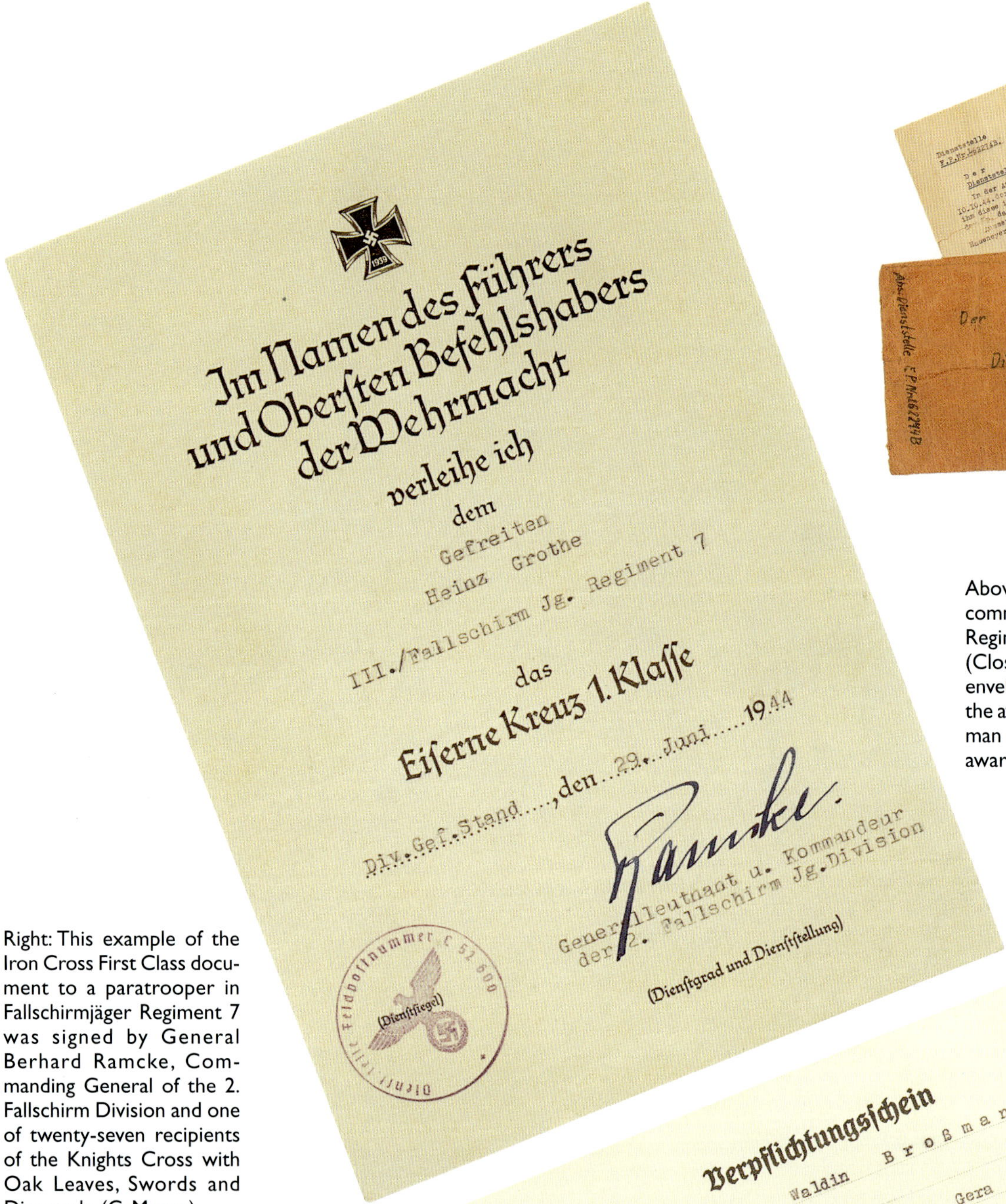

Im Namen des Führers
und Obersten Befehlshabers
der Wehrmacht
verleihe ich
dem
Gefreiten
Heinz Grothe
III./Fallschirm Jg. Regiment 7
das
Eiserne Kreuz 1. Klasse
Div.Gef.Stand....,den..29..Juni.....1944
Generalleutnant u. Kommandeur
der 2. Fallschirm Jg. Division
(Dienstgrad und Dienststellung)
(Dienstsiegel)

Right: This example of the Iron Cross First Class document to a paratrooper in Fallschirmjäger Regiment 7 was signed by General Berhard Ramcke, Commanding General of the 2. Fallschirm Division and one of twenty-seven recipients of the Knights Cross with Oak Leaves, Swords and Diamonds. (C. Mason)

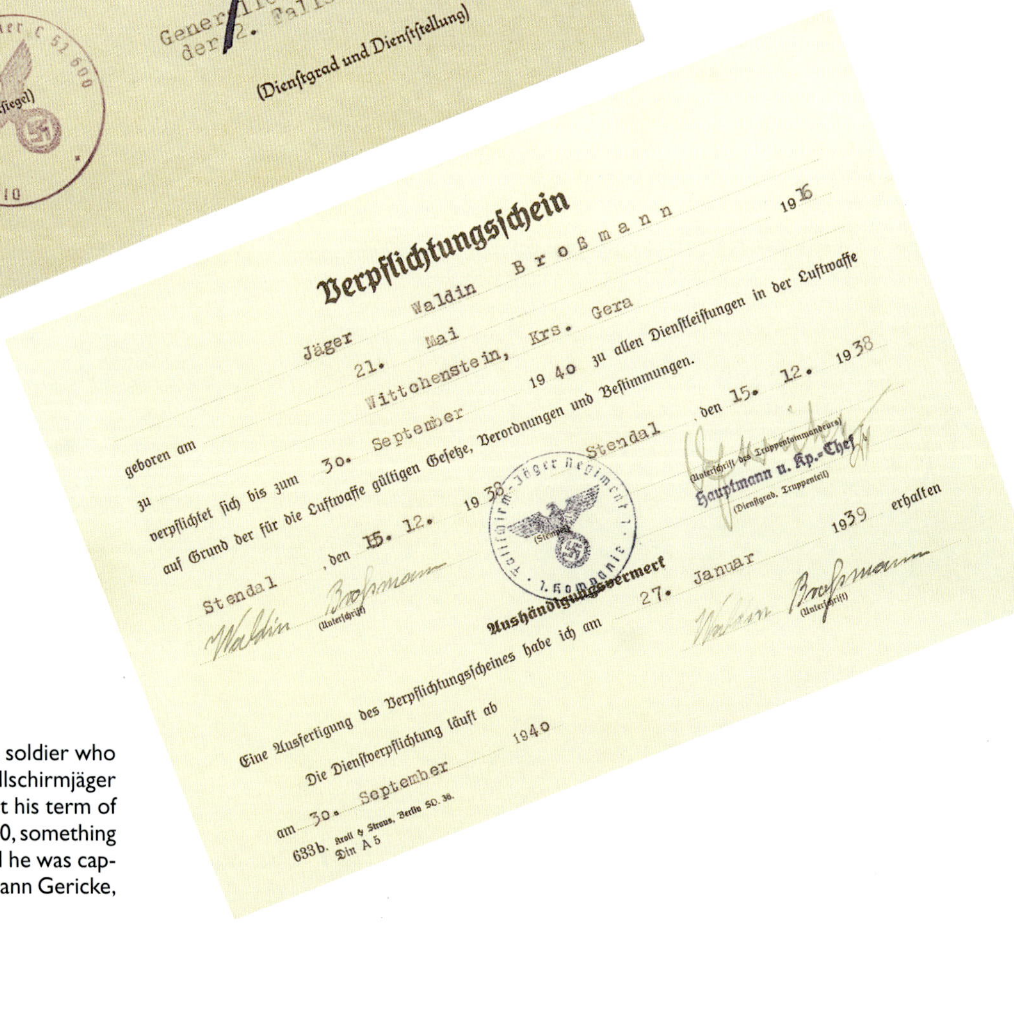

Verpflichtungsschein
Jäger Waldin Broßmann
geboren am 21. Mai 1916
zu Wittchenstein, Krs. Gera
verpflichtet sich bis zum 30. September 1940 zu allen Dienstleistungen in der Luftwaffe
auf Grund der für die Luftwaffe gültigen Gesetze, Verordnungen und Bestimmungen.
Stendal, den 15. 12. 1938
(Unterschrift)
Stendal, den 15. 12. 1938
(Unterschrift des Truppenkommandeurs)
Hauptmann u. Kp.-Chef
(Dienstgrad, Truppenteil)
Aushändigungsvermerk
Eine Ausfertigung des Verpflichtungsscheines habe ich am 27. Januar 1939 erhalten
(Unterschrift)
Die Dienstverpflichtung läuft ab
am 30. September 1940
633b. Kroll & Straus, Berlin SO. 36.
Din A 5

Right: An example of the enlistment papers to a soldier who was about to become a member of the 1st Fallschirmjäger Regiment, dated December 15, 1938. Note that his term of enlistment was to expire on September 30, 1940, something which did not happen as this soldier fought until he was captured in Italy. The document is signed by Hauptmann Gericke, commander of the 1st company. (Willi Zahn)

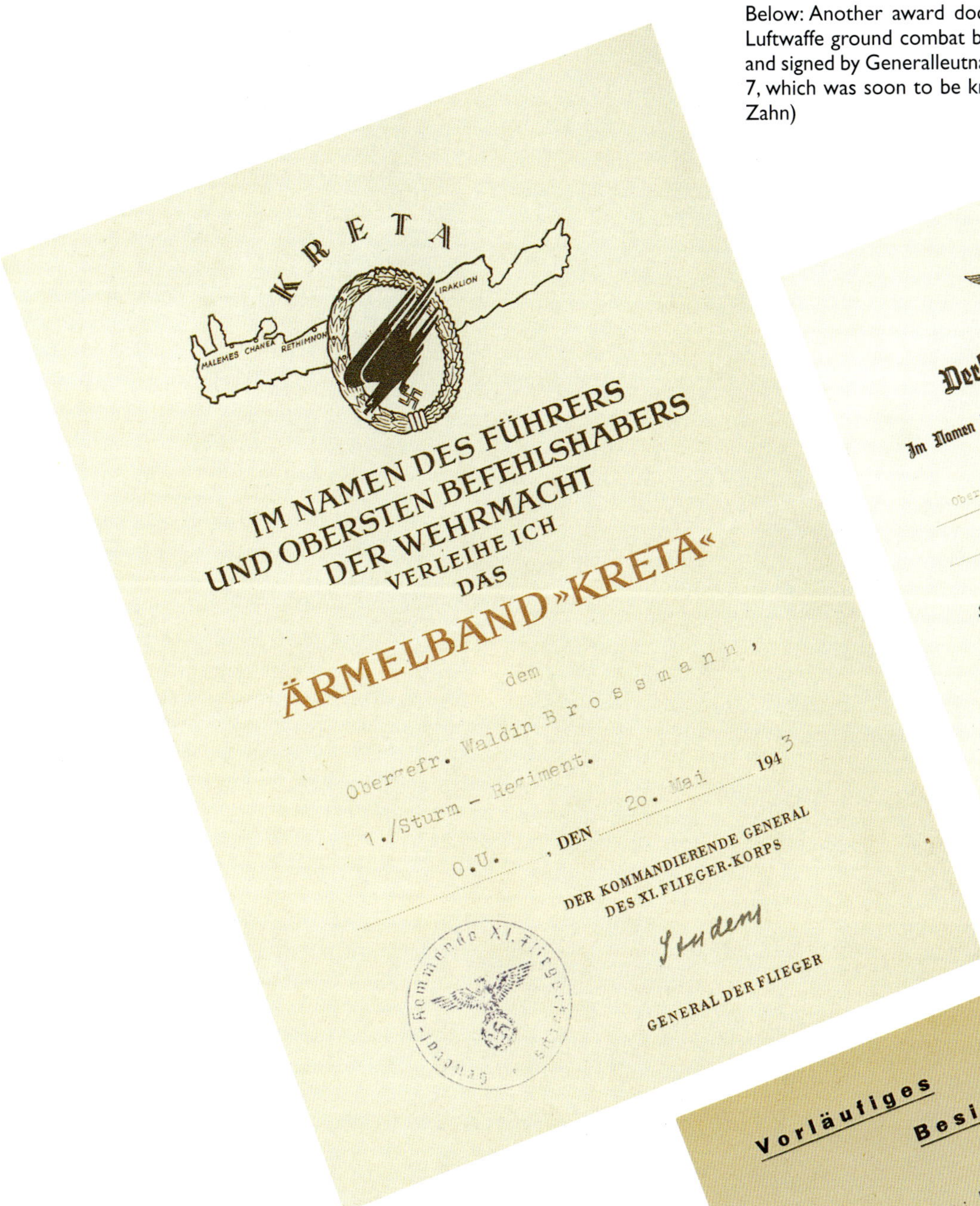
KRETA

MALEMES CHANEA RETHIMNON IRAKLION

IM NAMEN DES FÜHRERS
UND OBERSTEN BEFEHLSHABERS
DER WEHRMACHT
VERLEIHE ICH
DAS

ÄRMELBAND »KRETA«

dem

Oberefr. Waldin Brossmann,

1./Sturm - Regiment.

O.U. , DEN 20. Mai 1943

DER KOMMANDIERENDE GENERAL
DES XI. FLIEGER-KORPS

Student

GENERAL DER FLIEGER

Above: This document awards the Kreta campaign cufftitle to the same soldier, this time as a member of the 1st company of the Sturm Regiment. Award documents are unique in that they associate names, with battles. (Willi Zahn)

Below: Another award document to the same soldier, this time for the Luftwaffe ground combat badge while still serving in the Sturm Regiment, and signed by Generalleutnant Heidrich, the commander of Flieger Division 7, which was soon to be known as the 1st Fallschirmjäger Division. (Willi Zahn)

Verleihungsurkunde

Im Namen des Oberbefehlshabers der Luftwaffe
verleihe ich dem

Obergefreiten Waldin Brossmann,

1./Sturm-Regiment,

das

Erdkampfabzeichen der Luftwaffe

O.U., den 7. 7. 1942

Heidrich

Generalleutnant
und Divisionskommandeur

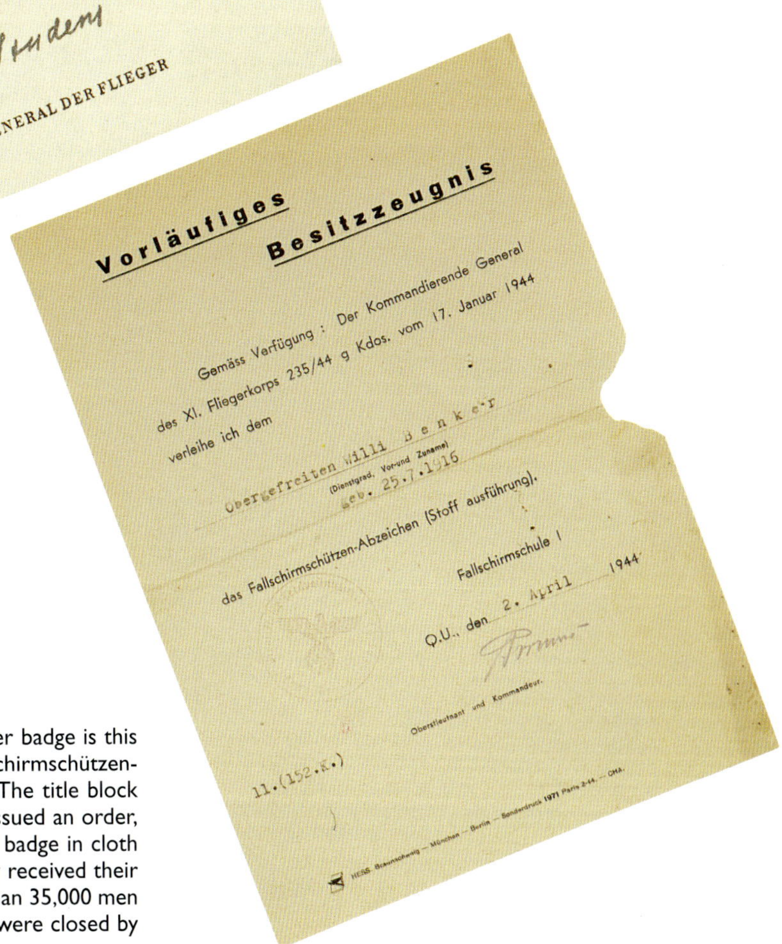
Vorläufiges Besitzzeugnis

Gemäss Verfügung : Der Kommandierende General
des XI. Fliegerkorps 235/44 g Kdos. vom 17. Januar 1944
verleihe ich dem

Obergefreiten Willi Henker
(Dienstgrad, Vor- und Zuname)
geb. 25.7.1916

das Fallschirmschützen-Abzeichen (Stoff ausführung).

Fallschirmschule I

O.U., den 2. April 1944

Oberstleutnant und Kommandeur.

11.(152.K.)

Right: One of the rarest of the award document styles for the paratrooper badge is this "Vorläufiges Besitzzeugnis," or "preliminary authorization" to wear the Fallschirmschützen-abzeichen in cloth given on April 2, 1944 by Fallschirmschule I (Stendal). The title block seems to indicate that the Commanding General of the XI Fliegerkorps issued an order, number 235/44 g Kdos, on 17 January 1944 authorizing the award of the badge in cloth upon completion of jump school. Prior to that, men had to wait until they received their badges at their units in an award ceremony to wear the badge. No more than 35,000 men were trained as jumpers during the Third Reich, and all the jump schools were closed by early fall 1944. (C. Mason)

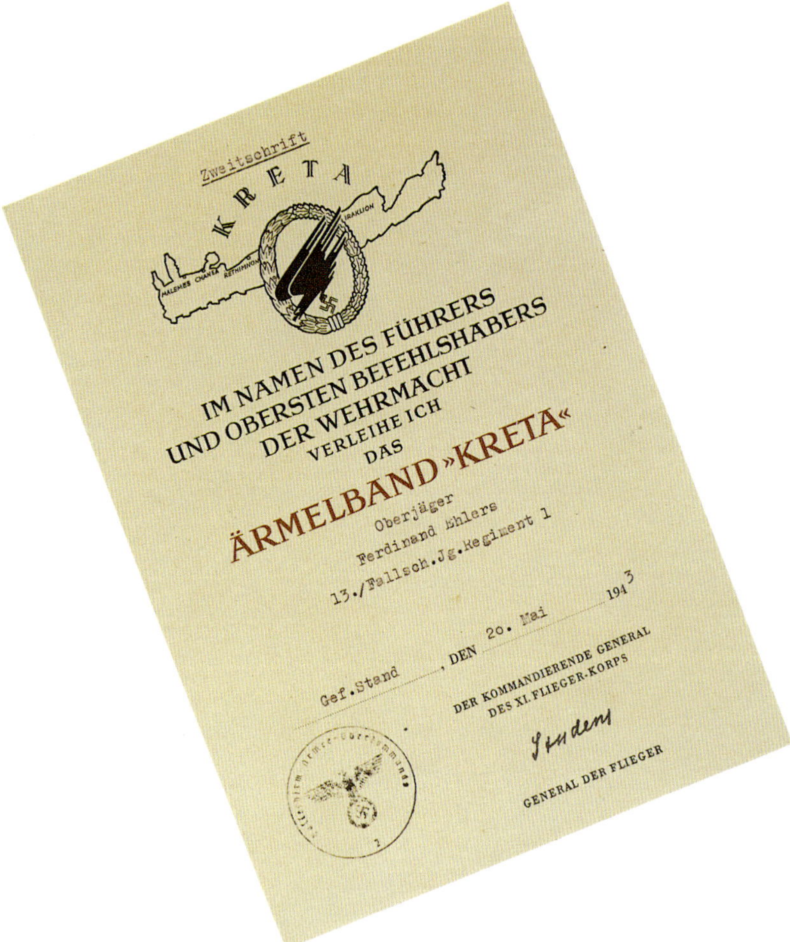
Zweitschrift

KRETA

IM NAMEN DES FÜHRERS
UND OBERSTEN BEFEHLSHABERS
DER WEHRMACHT
VERLEIHE ICH
DAS

ÄRMELBAND »KRETA«

Oberjäger
Ferdinand Ehlers
13./Fallsch.Jg.Regiment 1

Gef.Stand, DEN 20. Mai 1943

DER KOMMANDIERENDE GENERAL
DES XI. FLIEGER-KORPS

GENERAL DER FLIEGER

Left: Paratroopers and army personnel who made a landing on Crete by parachute, glider, aircraft or small boat, as well as airmen and sailors in the combat zone between May 20 and May 27, 1941 received the Kreta campaign cufftitle. The small group of last reserves who jumped on May 28 were excluded. This two-color award document to Oberjäger Ferdinand Ehlers is the type given to Fallschirmjäger. The award date, May 20, 1943 (two years to the day after the initial assault), is typical. (C. Mason)

Above: Oberjäger Ferdinand Ehlers, who was also engaged in the Narvik operation, stands at the far right. (C. Mason)

Einschreiben

Familie
Oertel
Chemnitz / Sa.
Berndorferstr. 187

Dienststelle L 33344
LG.P.A. Paris

Einschreiben

Dienststelle L 33344 O.U., den 30.5.43
Luftgaupostamt Paris

Familie
Oertel
Chemnitz / Sa.
Berndorferstr. 187

In der Anlage überreicht Ihnen die Kompanie für Ihren Sohn Gerhard das Ärmelband Kreta. Die Kompanie beglückwünscht Ihren Sohn zu dieser Auszeichnung.
Gleichzeitig erhalten Sie die Ostmedaille, die ihm am 4.7.42 verliehen worden ist.

Anlagen: Ärmelband
Ostmedaille
2 Urkunden

Hauptmann u. Kp.-Chef

IM NAMEN DES FÜHRERS
UND
OBERSTEN BEFEHLSHABERS
DER WEHRMACHT
IST DEM

Obergefreiten Gerhard Oertel

AM 4. 7. 1942

DIE MEDAILLE
WINTERSCHLACHT IM OSTEN
1941/42
(OSTMEDAILLE)
VERLIEHEN WORDEN.

FÜR DIE RICHTIGKEIT:
Oberstleutnant u. Rgt.-Führer

The document for the Winterschlacht im Osten (Russian Front) medal is not rare but is not found to Fallschirmjäger as often as other awards, primarily because of the limited number of paratroopers at that stage of the war. Because Fallschirmjäger units were never named on this document, the only indicator is the unit stamp. This example was mailed with best wishes from his Kompanie to the recipient's family in Chemnitz, together with the document for the Kreta cufftitle and both awards. (C. Mason)

Im Namen des Führers und Obersten Befehlshabers der Wehrmacht

verleihe ich dem

Gefreiten

Ernst Müller

das

Eiserne Kreuz 2. Klasse

Iraklion, den 29. Mai 1941

(Dienstsiegel)

Oberst u. Rgt. Kommandeur

(Dienstgrad und Dienststellung)

Above: This document for the Iron Cross Second Class is one of the most common award documents found to Fallschirmjäger. This one is notable in that it was signed by Oberst Bruno Brauer. Brauer was the first Fallschirmjäger and carried Fallschirmschützenschein #1. In 1943 and 1944, Brauer returned to Crete and served as the Governor General of the island. Although he acted in accordance with the Geneva Convention, he was arrested after the war by the Greek government and tried before a kangaroo court. In one of the more egregious cases of post-war revenge, Brauer was put to death in 1947 for his role as Governor General. He rests today with his men in the graveyard on Hill 107 above Maleme. (C. Mason)

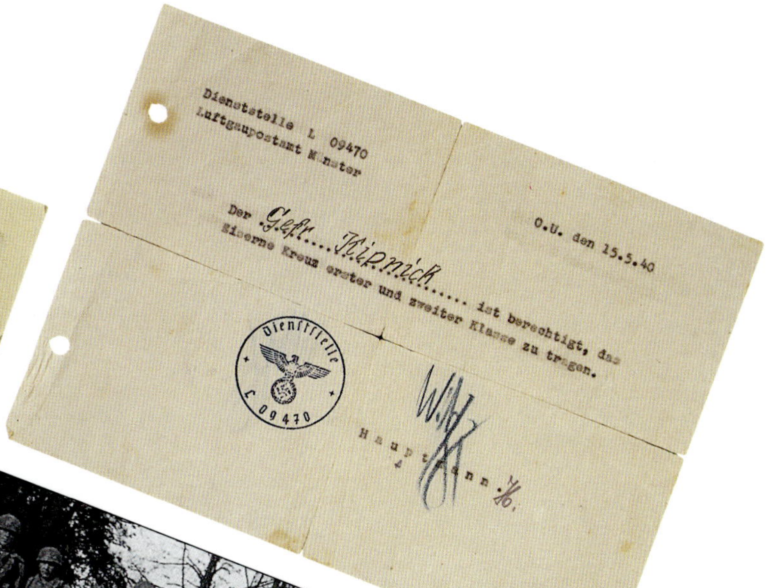

Dienststelle L 09470
Luftgaupostamt Münster

O.U. den 15.5.40

Der Gefr. Kipnick ist berechtigt, das Eiserne Kreuz erster und zweiter Klasse zu tragen.

Dienststelle L 09470

Hauptmann

Top: An unusual example of the provisional award of the Iron Cross 1st and 2nd Class to Gefreiter Kipnick for valor in the glider assault on Eben Emael several days after the attack and signed by the legendary Rudolf Witzig, who earned the Knights Cross in the action. The rubber stamp is that of the Fallschirmjäger Pioneer Zug, the designation at that time for the assault group which captured the fortress. (C. Mason)

Above: In this photograph taken shortly after the surrender of the Belgian garrison at Eben Emael, Gefreiter Kipnick stands third from the right. (C. Mason)

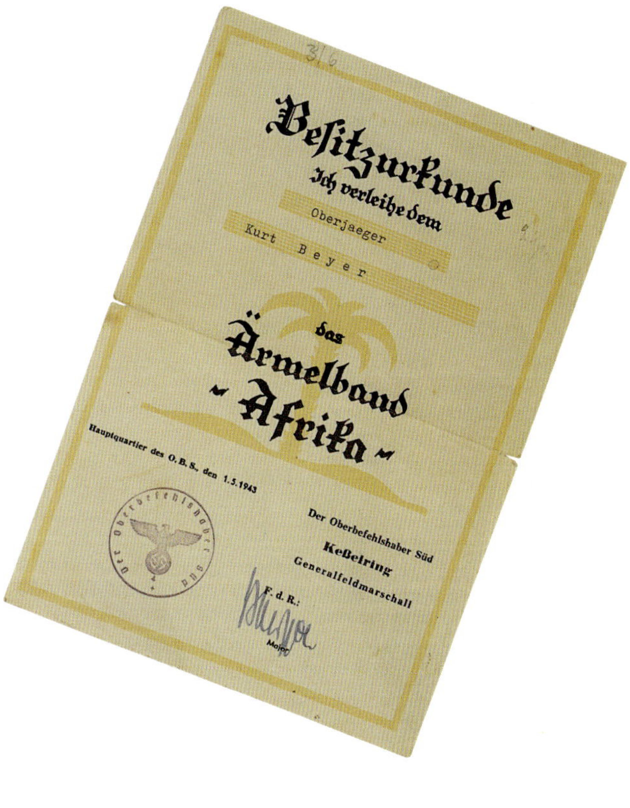

Besitzurkunde

Ich verleihe dem

Oberjaeger

Kurt Beyer

das

Ärmelband „Afrika"

Hauptquartier des O.B.S., den 1.5.1943

Der Oberbefehlshaber Süd
Kesselring
Generalfeldmarschall

F.d.R.:

Major

Right: Typical example of the document for the Afrika Cufftitle awarded to a Fallschirmjäger, in this case, Oberjäger Kurt Beyer. The document has the facsimile signature of Generalfeldmarschall Kesselring. (C. Mason)

Vorläufiges Besitzzeugnis

Der Führer
und Oberste Befehlshaber
der Wehrmacht

hat

dem Leutnant Friedrich Bausch

das Ritterkreuz
des Eisernen Kreuzes

am 12.3.1945 verliehen.

Gef.Stand, den 21.3.1945.

Oberst und Divisionsführer.

Above: The Knights Cross award document given to Leutnant Friedrich Bausch on 12 March 1945 while serving as the Kompanie Chef of the 3.Kompanie, Fallschirm Pioneer Bataillon 5. The award was prepared in the field on the back of a flight manifest and signed by the divisional commander, Oberst Kurt Gröschke. The medal is a typical example of a field expedient Knights Cross made from an Iron Cross 2nd Class. (C. Mason)

Im Namen des Führers
und Obersten Befehlshabers
der Wehrmacht

verleihe ich
dem

Fw. Karl v. Gutowski
13./Sturm-Regiment

das
Eiserne Kreuz 2. Klasse

O.U., den 11.6. 1941.

(Dienststempel)

(Dienstgrad und Dienststellung)

Right: Typical example of the document for the Iron Cross 2nd Class. This specimen is to a Feldwebel in the 13. Kompanie of the Sturm Regiment for action on Crete and is signed by Eugen "Papa" Meindl. (C. Mason)

VORLÄUFIGE BESITZURKUNDE

Nr. 54306

Der

Obgefr. Zeissig Hans

geb. 30.8.22, hat den 54/44 Fallschirmschützen-Lehrgang in der Zeit vom 10.4. bis 30.4.44 bei der Fallschirmschule II mit Erfolg bestanden. Auf Befehl des Komm. Generals, General d. Flieger Student, wurde dem

Obgefr. Zeissig

das Fallschirmschützen-Abzeichen (in Stoff) als Zeichen der Anerkennung verliehen

Wittstock, den 30.4.1944

8213 Sonderdruck Gustav Kühn, Neuruppin

Left: This certificate was awarded towards the end of the war upon completion of jump school. It authorizes the bearer to wear the Fallschirmschützenabzeichen in cloth. The right hand side is exactly the size of a Soldbuch page, and was intended to be pasted into the bearer's Soldbuch, although no examples have been seen of this in practice. The left hand side was intended to provide inspiration to the new Fallschirmjäger, but at a postwar reunion one veteran noted wryly it was generally found useful on the next trip to the latrine. (C. Mason)

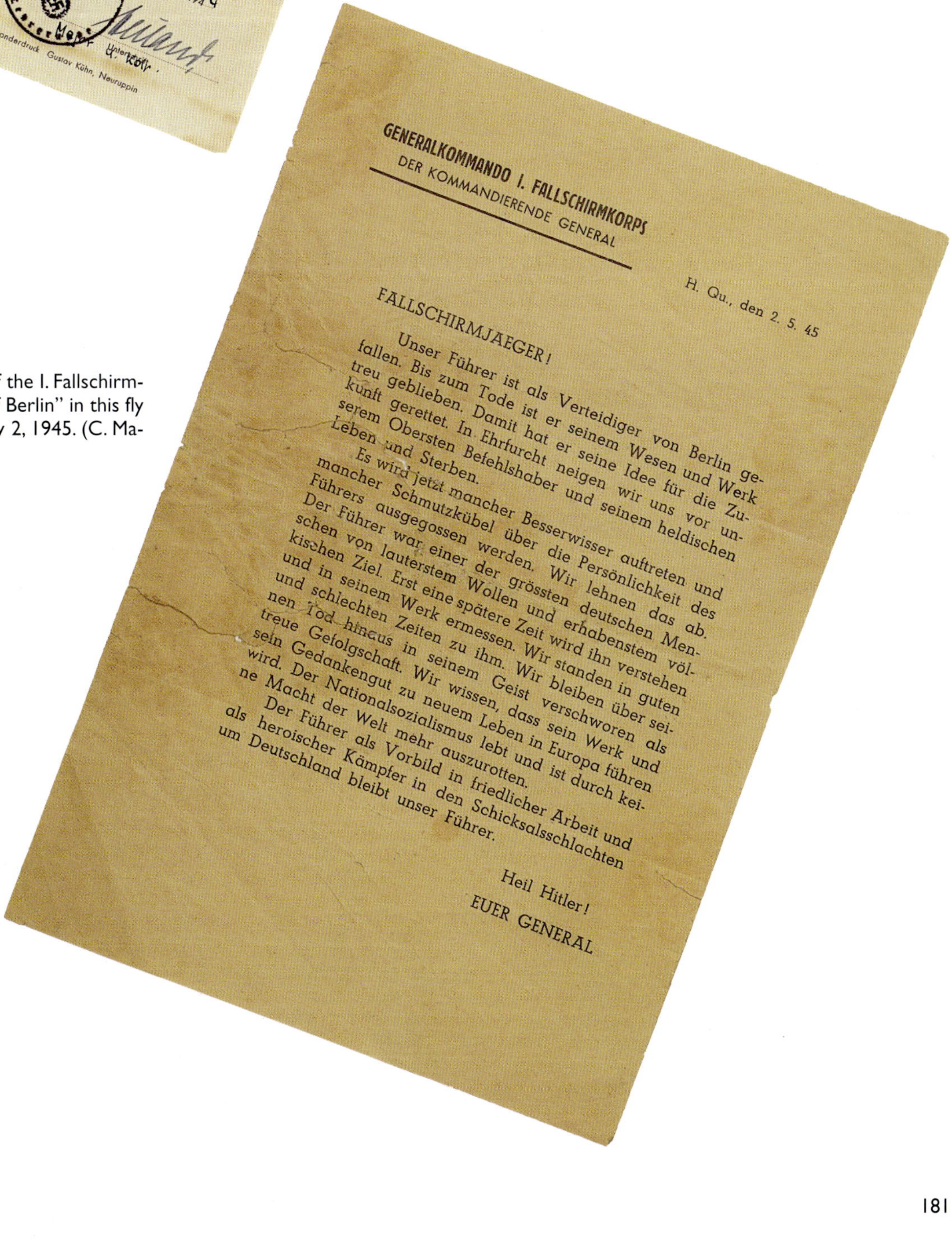

GENERALKOMMANDO I. FALLSCHIRMKORPS
DER KOMMANDIERENDE GENERAL

H. Qu., den 2. 5. 45

FALLSCHIRMJAEGER!

Unser Führer ist als Verteidiger von Berlin gefallen. Bis zum Tode ist er seinem Wesen und Werk treu geblieben. Damit hat er seine Idee für die Zukunft gerettet. In Ehrfurcht neigen wir uns vor unserem Obersten Befehlshaber und seinem heldischen Leben und Sterben.

Es wird jetzt mancher Besserwisser auftreten und mancher Schmutzkübel über die Persönlichkeit des Führers ausgegossen werden. Wir lehnen das ab. Der Führer war einer der grössten deutschen Menschen von lauterstem Wollen und erhabenstem völkischen Ziel. Erst eine spätere Zeit wird ihn verstehen und in seinem Werk ermessen. Wir standen in guten und schlechten Zeiten zu ihm. Wir bleiben über seinen Tod hinaus in seinem Geist verschworen als treue Gefolgschaft. Wir wissen, dass sein Werk und sein Gedankengut zu neuem Leben in Europa führen wird. Der Nationalsozialismus lebt und ist durch keine Macht der Welt mehr auszurotten.

Der Führer als Vorbild in friedlicher Arbeit und als heroischer Kämpfer in den Schicksalsschlachten um Deutschland bleibt unser Führer.

Heil Hitler!

EUER GENERAL

Right: After Hitler's suicide, the members of the I. Fallschirmkorps learned of his death as a "defender of Berlin" in this fly sheet from the CG of the Korps dated May 2, 1945. (C. Mason)

Left: One of many propaganda postcards which depicted the Fallschirmjäger in action. Considerable artist license shows the men in the foreground carrying weapons, although those still in the air or landing aren't carrying any. (C. Mason)

Above left: Many humorous postcards were also produced. This early card depicts Fallschirmjäger dressed like pilots. The writing is in old Sutterlin script, which was phased out during the Third Reich. Germans born since the war cannot read it. (C. Mason)

Above: Another humorous postcard shows a Fallschirmjäger dropping in on a Flak man making time with a girl for a Winterhilfswerk contribution. (C. Mason)

Left: Another very rare Fallschirmjäger postcard is this card produced for the troops of the 6. Fallschirm Division to use as a Christmas card in 1944. The sketch was done by one of the division's own soldiers. The tactical symbol of the 6. Fallschirm Division, a sword superimposed over a diving eagle on a shield, appears in the lower left of the card. (C. Mason)

Below: A rare Fallschirmjäger postcard bearing the badge and a poem written by a paratrooper. (C. Mason)

Above right: A typical example of a postcard sent from one of the four jump schools. Each school had a distinctive rubber stamp which it applied to outgoing postcards as a souvenir. This stamp reads "Fallschirmschule Wittstock 3. Schülerkompanie Briefstempel." It was sent from Wittstock to a young woman on September 4, 1941. (C. Mason)

Right: First day covers were popular with stamp collectors even in the Third Reich. This card was one of a series depicting military flags. It was canceled in Dresden on April 20, 1941. (C. Mason)

Below: This postcard shows Major Koch, the commander of the assault force which seized Eben Emäl. (Willi Zahn)

Above: Scores of postcards with a Fallschirmjäger theme were produced in the Third Reich. Most are fairly common. This portrait of General Ramcke, however, is rarely seen. (C. Mason)

Above right: A series of post cards were put out early in the war depicting famous paratroopers. This card depicts a pioneer (or engineer) of Sturm Abteilung Koch, the victors of Eben Emäl and was painted by the famous German war artist Wolfgang Willich. (Willi Zahn)

Above: This card depicts Oberst Bräuer during the campaign in Holland in 1940. He was the commander of the 1st Fallschirmjäger Regiment at that time. (Willi Zahn)

Left: Another famous member of the forces which assaulted Eben Emäl was Feldwebel Arpke. (Willi Zahn)

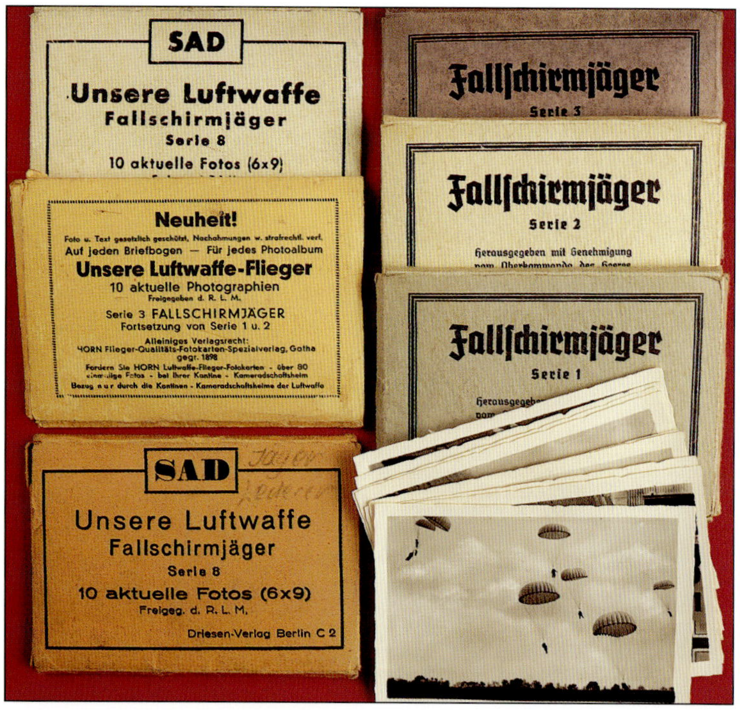

Every jump school and home garrison had a soldier's canteen in which enlisted men could relax, play cards, drink beer and buy toiletries and small items. Souvenir photos of jump school training were popular for scrapbooks and photo albums. The photos usually came in packets of ten and measured about 2" x 3". Some of the variations are seen here. (C. Mason)

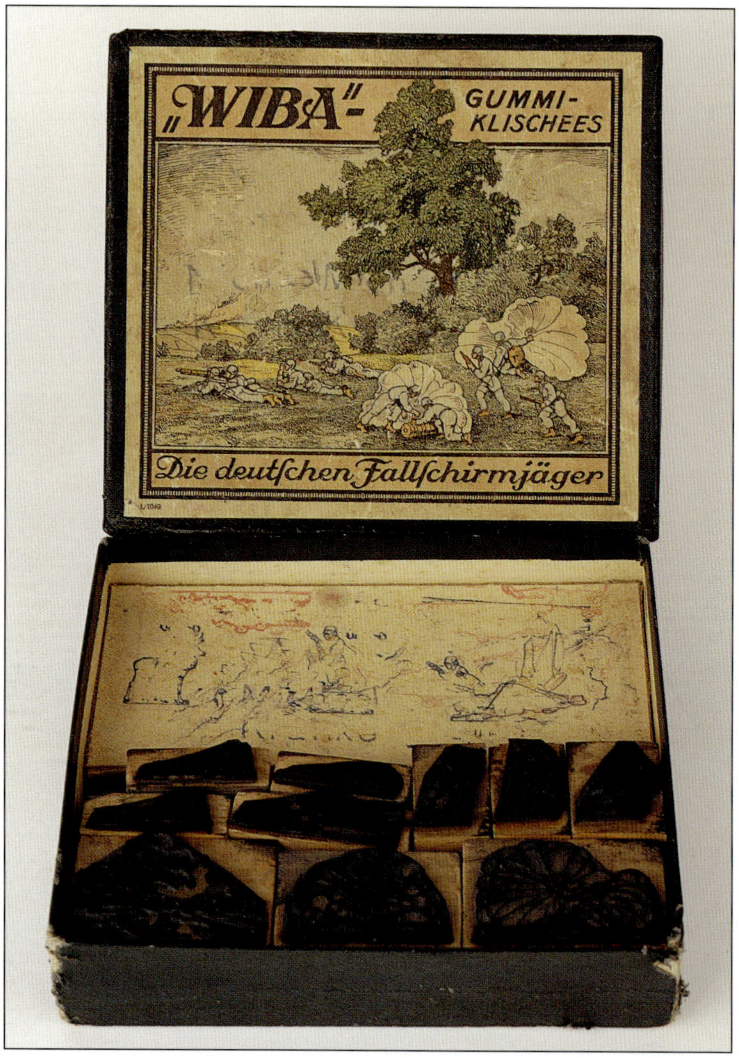

Above: The "young lions" of the Fallschirmjäger appeared in newsreels, magazines, books, even children's games. This is a children's game dating to about 1940. Note the swastika on the tail fin of the aircraft. (C. Mason)

Below: Inside the Fallschirmjäger Spiel was a game board with target holes, two aircraft, and two weighted Fallschirmjäger figures. Using the aircraft as flippers, players would try to score points by flipping their paratroopers into the high-scoring holes. (C. Mason)

Left: The élan and success of the German paratroops were widely publicized in Nazi Germany, and the Fallschirmjäger quickly became part of popular culture. This is a child's toy in the form of a group of rubber stamps which could be used to make endless battles on paper. (C. Mason)

Service mementos, such as this decorative glazed ceramic tile for the test section of the 11. Flieger Korps (a code name for the Fallschirm-Korps), were popular as souvenirs with the troops. This piece was designed as a wall hanging. (C. Mason)

Two examples of the plaque given for recognition of exemplary service during the battle of Crete in their leather and velvet frames. The plaque is made of cast iron. The award on the left was made to Fallschirmjäger-Feuerwerker Ewald Bilitski for moving explosives out of a burning supply dump. His specialty would be translated today as "Explosive Ordnance Disposal." (Each Fallschirmjäger regiment had one or two such experts on the regimental staff.) This award is roughly equivalent to the U.S. Bronze Star without Combat "V." Other versions of this plaque are postwar copies. (C. Mason)

Commemorative beer mug presented to the surviving members the III. Bataillon of Fallschirmjäger Regiment 1 by the town of Gardelegen after their return from Crete in the summer of 1941. The front bears the inscription "To The Victors of Crete" ("Den Siegern von Kreta") while the reverse depicts the town's landmark, the Salzwedeler Tor. Mugs may have been symbolic also of the famous brewery located in the town, one of the oldest in Germany at the time. The mug on the right was presented to Oberjäger Wilhelm Reinhardt, 9. Kompanie, FJR1. (C. Mason)

Right: Luftwaffe Honor Salver for Bravery. Very scarce award for bravery presented only to "non-flying" personnel. It is produced of genuine silver and has the Reichsmarshall Göring insignia in the center. This example was presented to Hugo Paul, a paratrooper with a highly distinguished service record. The inscription translates, "In Recognition of Distinguished Achievements in Action." (Collection of Wes Bray) Above right: Rear view showing the rear of the design and the manufacturer/silversmith's data and trademark, "Feinsilber Alpaka Auflage Joh. Wagner & Sohne."

Luftwaffe Standarte. Truly one of the most beautiful flags to be produced during the Third Reich; this was the 4' x 4' (approximate size) "Regimental Standarte." This particular example with a yellow/gold background is for a Flight or Paratrooper unit. Notice the incredible detail in the silver bullion designs. (Collection of Bill Shea, "The Ruptured Duck")

The opposite side portrays in spectacular detail an Iron Cross in the center with four streams of bullion and silk reaching out to each of the corners ending in a swastika. These were hand-produced by groups of seamstresses working together.

The flag of a Fallschirmjäger regimental commander. It is stretched over a wire frame and originally had a celluloid covering to protect it. (C. Mason)

Above: Cased Luftwaffe Standard Bearer's Gorget. This half-moon shaped breast plate was worn suspended by a chain and is made of matte silver with a handsome burnished silver eagle clutching the swastika in a wreath over a series of flags. This example is in its original black cardboard storage box with the cover (not shown). (Collection of Bill Shea, "The Ruptured Duck")

Right: The chain is finished in the same matte silver as the gorget itself. The reverse (not shown) is covered in a blue/grey wool cloth and has a metal tang with the name of the manufacturer.

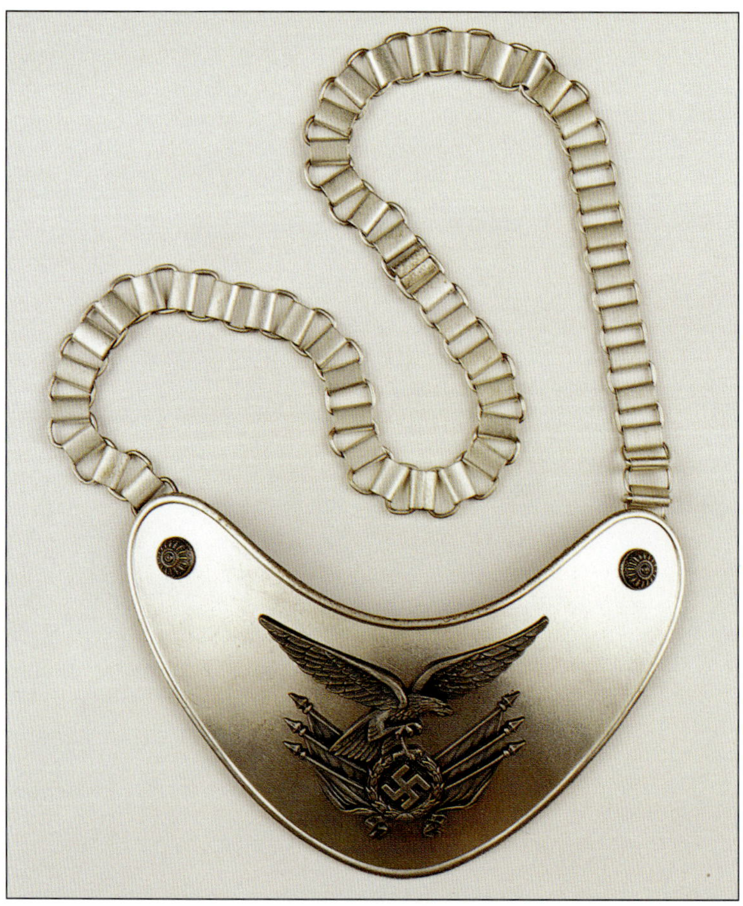

Above: Luftwaffe Flag Pole Top. Front view of a handsome nickel plated pole top and "wing tip" protectors. This was for the Regimental "Standarte" and would slide over the pole itself. The leather cone-shaped protectors would slip over the ends of the wings when the flag was not being displayed. (Collection of Bill Shea, "The Ruptured Duck")

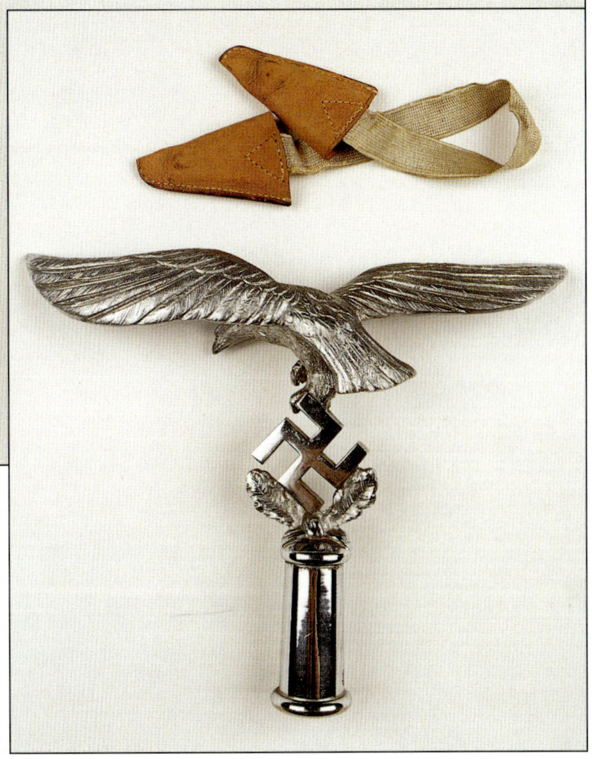

Right: Rear view showing the fine workmanship and great attention to detail.

Above: Baby's cradle presented to families of paratroopers from the 3rd Fallschirmjäger Regiment (3rd Paratrooper Rgt) when they had a child. The cradle itself is made of a bird's eye maple. Each side has distinctive writing or characters. This side features an Adolf Hitler quote which translates, "The Child is the most valuable possession of a People." (Collection of Bill Shea, "The Ruptured Duck")

Right: This side shows the actual Paratrooper badge and has a quote surrounding it which translates, "Red Shines the Sun." Under this is the name of the unit, Parachute Regiment 3.

Above: This side has views of the city of Braunschweig, where the unit was from (Brunswick).

Right: This side details the birth of 1st Lieutenant Walter Pagel's (and his wife Ilse) first child (Weibke) who was born on the 12th of November 1940 in Brunsbuttel-koog.

Chapter Six

Other Axis Airborne

Italian Paratrooper Recruiting Poster. Highly symbolic and colorful poster depicting a well armed Italian RSI paratrooper in action. The caption translates, "Stormtroop Paratroopers; Republican Airforce." During the RSI period, the Arditi belonged to the Airforce and were specially trained and highly skilled in commando-type raids behind enemy lines. (Collection of Bill Shea, "The Ruptured Duck")

Opposite -
LEFT: World War II Italian Paratrooper Rig. This front view all "kitted" out depicts an Italian 2nd Lieutenant wearing a grey-green wool special Army Paratrooper Model 1941 tunic without shoulder boards or collar lapels. He wears Officer's gold bullion collar tabs. This photo also shows an excellent view of the "other ranks" tunic with two pleated chest pockets and two unpleated lower pockets. It also has a wool waist belt (hidden by the brown leather Officer's belt). Obviously this 2nd Lieutenant still utilized his "other ranks" tunic. The straight legged (bloused at the ankles) combat trousers are shown. There is also an excellent view of the special Model 1941-42 Paratrooper helmet with nose protector (paramaso). This was more commonly referred to as the "sausage" and was made of green-grey leather. The Model 1942 camouflage cloth cover is also worn.

RIGHT: Rear view showing the type 35 gas bag as well as the rare canvas paratrooper jump bag for carrying the MAB 38 Beretta machine gun during a combat jump. Extra ammunition magazines, tools and spare parts as well as the sub-machinegun could be carried in the pouches. Note the rear view of the special Model 1941-42 Paratrooper helmet. (Collection of Bill Shea, "The Ruptured Duck")

View of left sleeve showing the officer's gold bullion parachute and the rare Arditi badge which indicates that the wearer has gone through training as a Stormtrooper. This entire paratrooper set up reflects the Republica Sociale Italiana (RSI) period (after September 1943).

This view of the left sleeve indicates that the wearer was wounded in combat.

This view of the right cuff area (also the same for the left cuff area) depicts the gold bullion rank insignia for a 2nd Lieutenant. These are also for the RSI period (after September of 1943) as prior to this the Royal Army used a loop rather than a diamond shape over the gold stripe.

Frontal view of chest area clearly showing some of the distinctive characteristics of the specially produced grey-green wool Sahariana style Model 1941 tunic. This photo also shows the handsome silver and gold bullion collar insignia for paratroopers.

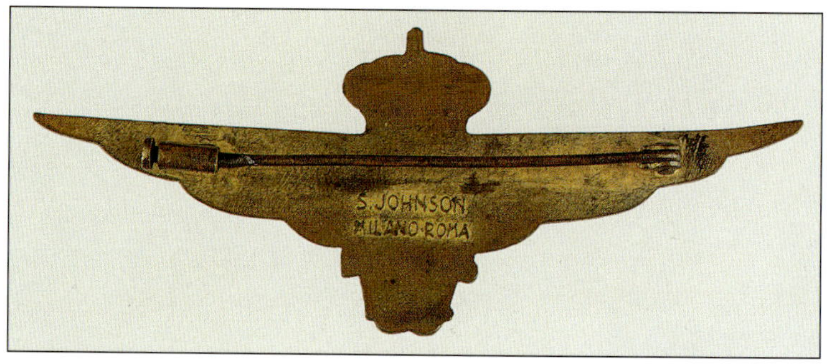

Left: Italy's paratroops are well known to historians. Both the Folgore and the Nembo divisions had good combat records. This is the first badge awarded to Italian army paratroopers. The design incorporates a sword and the Italian fascist symbol on either side of the enameled parachute. Right: The reverse of the Italian parachutist badge shows the unique pin device and the maker mark, "S Johnson Milano Roma." (C. Mason)

Italian paratroops exit the SM 82 "Marsupiale" using the 1F41SP parachute. (Richards)

Italian paratrooper set to make a practice jump with Salvator D39 rig. (Richards)

Italian led Libyan paratroops form up wearing Salvator D37 rigs. (Richards)

Germany and Italy were not the only members of the Axis in Europe to field paratroops against the Allies. Hungary established a jump school at Papa with personnel trained in Germany, and had a battalion which fought well on the Russian Front. Shown below are Hungarian paratroops in training.

The Master Hungarian parachutist badge (above) and the qualification badge for wear on the jump smock (below) are extremely rare and verification of their originality through comparison with known original specimens is difficult. There were fewer than 500 Hungarian paratroopers during World War II, and less than twenty qualified to wear the Master Parachutist badge. The origin of these badges is unknown.

Japanese army paratrooper rig. (Richards)

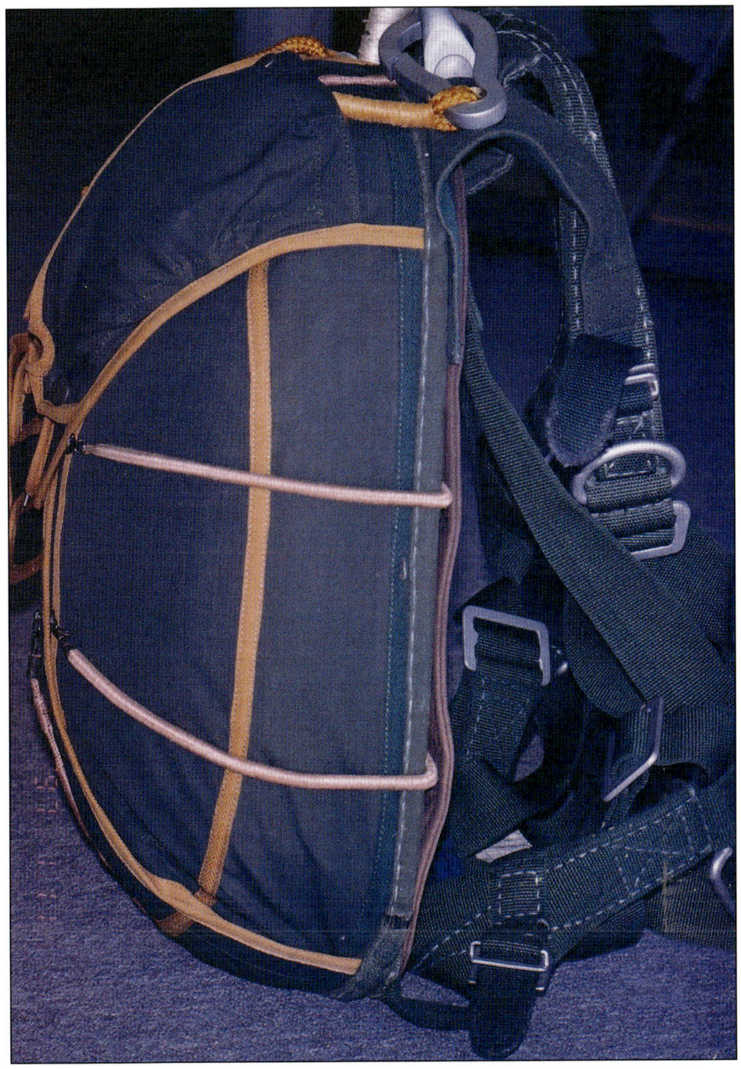

Side view of a Japanese naval parachute. (Richards)

Japanese army paratroops on board their aircraft prepared for a combat jump, 1944. (Richards)

Also from the Publisher

GERONIMO!: U.S. Airborne Uniforms, Insignia & Equipment in World War II. *Bill Rentz.* This fully illustrated volume explores the uniforms, insignia, and equipment of American Airborne, Glider, Troop Carrier, and Airborne Engineers in World War II. Included are over 500 detailed, up-close images of individual items, and multi-side views of full combat rig, and over 100 World War II era color and black and white photos, most unpublished, showing the uniforms and equipment as worn by the troops. Covered in this extensive book are: dress uniforms; jump jackets and pants; headgear; boots; jump wings, unit patches and other insignia; Marine Corps airborne; Troop Carrier and Airborne Engineers; equipment, including parachutes, weapons, communications, and many rare and unusual items exclusive to airborne troops; and a comparative section with both British and German airborne gear. Geronimo! is a detailed look at the clothing and equipment of America's Finest, and is an important reference work for the airborne collector, reenactor, historian and veteran.
Size: 9" x 12" • over 630 color and b/w photographs • 192pp.
ISBN: 0-7643-0677-4 • hard cover • $69.95

FOR KING AND COUNTRY: British Airborne Uniforms, Insignia & Equipment in World War II • 1st Airborne Division • 6th Airborne Division • 1st Polish Independent Parachute Brigade. *Harlan Glenn.* For King and Country is the first in a series of in-depth studies which will cover the uniforms, equipment, insignia, weapons, vehicles, and personal items of the British and Commonwealth soldier of World War II. This initial volume covers the British Airborne soldier of the 1st and 6th Airborne Divisions, and the 1st Polish Independent Parachute Brigade. With over 540 color recreation, and detail photos and over 65 unpublished war era black and white photographs, the complete airborne rig is covered in great detail. For King and Country brings to life the British Airborne soldier as never before. Each branch of the Airborne is covered: included are the paratroops, glider troops, divisional and administrative departments, and the glider pilots, as well as those liaison and attached troops. For King and Country is an essential reference for any military enthusiast, collector, reenactor, modeler, and veteran.
Size: 9" x 12" • over 600 color and b/w photographs • 192 pp.
ISBN: 0-7643-0794-0 • hard cover • $59.95